MODERN ECONOMIC ISSUES

OTTO ECKSTEIN, Harvard University, General Editor

In this series the great public issues in economics are posed and put in perspective by original commentary and reprints of the most interesting and significant recent statements by experts in economics and government.

JOHN A. PINCUS, the editor of this volume in the Modern Economic Issues series, is an economist with the RAND Corporation. He is the author of *Trade, Aid and Development, Economic Aid and International Cost Sharing*, and the editor of *Methods of Industrial Development*.

RESHAPING THE WORLD ECONOMY

Rich Countries and Poor

RESHAPING THE WORLD ECONOMY

RICH COUNTRIES AND POOR

Edited by John A. Pincus

PRENTICE-HALL, Inc., Englewood Cliffs, N.J.

Library of Congress Catalog Card Number 68-14464.
Printed in the United States of America.

Current printing (last digit):
10 9 8 7 6 5 4 3 2

 P
 A
 TO   M
 R   I
 I   K
 CORINNE
 I
CATH
   E
  FROM
   I E
   N
DAVE

PREFACE

This is an introduction to the role of the world economy in the economic development of poor nations. This subject, although it covers only a small part of the social, political, and economic "universe" that affects the development process, is nonetheless vast in itself. It stretches from the pure theory of growth and trade, through the economic structure of rich and poor countries, to the immediate issues in aid and trade policy that recently faced the 122 governments assembled at the second session of the United Nations Conference on Trade and Development, convened at New Delhi in 1968.

The selections in this volume are a sampling of informed opinion on the major issues of theory and policy. As the reader will see, it is a field where experts disagree, and differences of opinion are often so wide as to be startling. The Introduction tries to set the issues in perspective, to help the reader understand how differences in assumptions about facts and behavior lead to very different policy prescriptions.

Because problems of population and nutrition loom so large in underdeveloped countries, I have included in the first section of this volume brief selections on these topics, even though, strictly speaking, they go beyond the self-assigned limits of this volume. The second section discusses trade and aid theories and practices. The final section reviews the major current policy issues.

John A. Pincus

CONTENTS

RESHAPING THE WORLD ECONOMY

Rich Countries and Poor

INTRODUCTION

INTERNATIONAL POLICIES FOR ECONOMIC DEVELOPMENT

John A. Pincus

Today we are all bound together more and more by the threads of material interest and by the community of fear and hope that unite a reluctant world. We all know that an event in what used to be the remotest corner of earth can within a few days bring everyone face to face with destruction. It remains an open question whether man will survive this community that the technology of war has imposed on us all.

But these bonds do not only take the form of the delicate balance of terror. The entire realm of human intercourse moves in the same direction, through communication by sound, symbol, and pictures; through the movement of men, goods, services, and the financial means of exchange; through the ability, in short, to transmit—fast, far, and massively—idea, fact, emotion, material progress, and destruction.

Economic links have developed as strongly as the strategic, cultural, and political ones. Trade has grown more rapidly in recent years than ever before. After the end of World War II, world merchandise exports were valued at about $50 billion; by 1968, their value was estimated at $211 billion.[1] In the same manner, the value of official foreign aid to underdeveloped countries, virtually nonexistent before the end of World War II, rose from an average of $2 billion annually in the early fifties to $7.4 billion by 1968. United States foreign private investment, representative of the third major element of international economic relations, has similarly gone up from an annual rate of $4.8 billion in 1956 to $7.6 billion in 1966. All of these elements except the last rose much faster than the growth of combined national products or combined domestic investment during the same period.

A few simple examples illustrate the point. Before World War II, foreign cars were generally a luxury for the rich in the United States. Today, foreign makes account for more than 5 per cent of new car sales in the United States. Before World War II, many Latin American villagers

[1] Figures exclude trade between Communist countries.

might never have heard a radio. Today, Japanese transistors are commonplace in all but the remotest areas. Before World War II, middle class Parisians drank wine or cognac. Today, they have added Scotch whisky and Coke to the list. Before World War II, foreign aid was virtually unknown. Today, two dozen nations offer aid, a hundred receive it; Denmark has its own Peace Corps, and faraway Nepal, its corps of foreign advisors and its stock of aid-financed public works.

This increasing linkage of the world economy has brought people much closer together in material connections, dependence, and aspirations. But these links have not yet promoted the uniform growth of world prosperity. The world is still divided into rich and poor countries, and the rich countries' per capita incomes are growing faster and thereby widening the existing divisions.

This is obviously not an economic problem alone. From the viewpoint of the rich countries, it is often regarded as a political issue primarily affecting the peace of the world. Most of the warfare in the world over the past two decades has broken out in underdeveloped countries. Why do unrest, conflicts, and warfare so often erupt in the new nations of Asia, Africa, and Latin America? One factor, perhaps sometimes the major one, is the frustration and discontent created by poverty and by the awareness of being poor and "backward" in a world where many live in comfort.

Governments everywhere know that poverty and despair often breed violence, and most of them today take deliberate measures to raise living standards. The state's fight against poverty for its people is an old story. Bread for the people is a recurrent theme of ancient Rome's imperial history. In American life, there has been a perennial vision of a nation with no poor. A century ago, Western land seemed to offer this nation a promise of universal prosperity. In the decades of the 1930's through 1960's, under such slogans as New Deal, Fair Deal, New Frontier, and Great Society, the state has tried to promote both growth and a reparceling of shares in the country's income.

Some of these efforts have succeeded, and others have failed. Starvation and homelessness are now largely bitter memories in the United States, but poverty remains, and official estimates state that nearly 30 million Americans live below the poverty line.

Outside America on the world scene, there are about 3.3 billion citizens of earth. Most of them, about 2.3 billion, live in "economically underdeveloped" countries and are poor. China and India alone have 1.2 billion people, more than the *combined* populations of the 24 rich countries that make up North America, Western Europe, and Oceania plus the eight Communist nations of Eastern Europe. Most of these 2.3 billion residents of Asia, Africa, and Latin America live in poverty, often at bare subsistence levels. There are wealthy Indians, Colombians, Moroccans, just as there are poor Americans, Australians, and Swedes. But, by comparison, only a tiny proportion of the people in underdeveloped countries is even moderately well off.

Poverty is the rule, and affluence, the exception. There are enough resplendent maharajahs, dazzlingly wealthy rulers of Middle Eastern oil sheikhdoms, and South American latifundia owners to promote the prosperity of restaurateurs on the Riviera and bankers in Zurich, but they are few indeed, a gilding on the dunghills of poverty.

World poverty is not only widespread; it is also the dominant material fact of life for most people. Therefore, economic development is far from an exercise in economic or social theory alone; it is a vital issue of domestic and international politics worldwide.

The great gulf between the living standards of rich and poor countries injects the issue into world politics. In 1965, for example, the rich countries—North America, Western Europe, Japan, Australia, and New Zealand—("the North") had an average Gross National Product (GNP) per head of $2200 per year and a population of 588 million, while the less-developed countries—Africa, Latin America, and Asia, excluding Japan—("the South") excluding Mainland China, had a combined population of 1582 million with an average GNP per head of $190.[2] The North generally includes areas of temperate climate; most of its people are city dwellers. The South's people are largely tropical farmers, although its cities are growing fast. These less-developed countries (known for short as LDCs) of the South are referred to by the leaders of China as "the Country" which, according to Chinese ideology, will over the next century engulf "the Town," or the North.

This income gap that divides North and South is not only great, but it is also growing. Each year, per capita product in the rich countries grows about 17 times faster than in the poor countries. Sherwood Fine points out the crucial roles of population growth, natural resources, capital, skills, and government. Barbara Ward stresses the widening of the income gap and the historical, cultural, technological and psychological factors that need to be overcome if the South is to develop more rapidly.

Two of the biggest handicaps to narrowing the gap in living standards

[2] The use of dollars at official exchange rates to compare product per head exaggerates the gap somewhat. Obviously no one could survive at an annual income of $190 in the United States. The average value of "real" annual product per head in underdeveloped countries at United States prices is probably in the $300 to $400 range, perhaps one-sixth of the rich countries' average.

are the population explosion in the underdeveloped countries and the shortage of the food that will be needed to help poor people there reach decent standards of living. With the population of the South growing twice as fast as in the North, while its food output grows more slowly than the North's, the long-run specter of mass hunger is clearly genuine.

The world population problem and the world food problem are discussed in two articles written by committees advising President Johnson. In both cases, the authors point out how closely these issues are related to the vast and increasing differences between living standards in North and South.

CAN AID FILL THE GAP?

Mr. Fine's article was written in his capacity as an official of the Organization for Economic Cooperation and Development (OECD), the international organization that acts as a center for coordinating rich countries' foreign aid. It is natural that in his article he should assume that foreign aid is a vital element of international economic policy. But this is far from self-evident. International economic aid for less-developed countries is, relatively speaking, a novelty, dating back to the end of World War II. Previously, rich nations rarely, if ever, felt compelled to give large-scale aid to foreign countries. The obvious answer explaining the introduction of foreign aid is that it serves neocolonial or cold-war goals or the objectives of political and economic influence or domination, now that the great nineteenth-century colonial empires have vanished. However, the record of foreign aid hardly offers convincing evidence that aid is an effective political tool.

Some may question whether governments and people of the rich industrial countries should concern themselves with the well-being of the billions of people who live in the poor nations of Asia, Africa, and Latin America. Indeed, from the viewpoint of a nation's political or military self-interest as distinguished from ethical or charitable motives, there is no way to demonstrate that international aid for underdeveloped countries necessarily benefits the donors; there are always greater or lesser doubts. This is the reason that the size of the foreign aid bill is usually a controversial subject in rich countries.

Furthermore, economists do not even agree on whether foreign aid actually benefits poor countries. Milton Friedman has gone so far as to argue that foreign aid is harmful to economic development because, as a government-to-government flow, it increases the power of recipient governments to control economic life. The consequence, in Friedman's eyes, is to discourage private initiative and replace it with inefficient government-controlled economic activities removed from the disciplines of market competition. The results of foreign aid, he contends, are therefore adverse to freedom and democracy, as well as to economic growth. Friedman's views are strongly disputed by Charles Wolf, who states that government-to-government aid often serves to promote the economic interests of private business and to allow needed investments that private interests would be unable to finance.

American aid doctrines, however, are more political than economic in nature. The annual presidential foreign aid messages to Congress give the flavor—a blending of humanitarian concern and self-interest—of official American support of aid appropriations. The underlying argument is syllogistic: (1) a stable world favors American interests; (2) economic growth is conducive to stability; (3) foreign aid promotes economic growth; (4) therefore, the United States should offer foreign aid.

This argument has often been questioned, and contemporary analysis of foreign aid shows that reality is far more complex than the official syllogism implies.[3]

Even though official foreign aid flows are about $7 billion annually, it is clear that they are by themselves inadequate to fill the gap between the developing countries' economic aspirations and today's realities. The United Nations, in voting for a Development Decade in the 1960's, asked its wealthy members to contribute 1 per cent of national income to LDCs annually; but that target, which has been honored in the breach, would also be inadequate to meet those aspirations. And, for that matter, most people would not argue that aid should fill that gap. If developing countries need, on the average, to quadruple per capita income to achieve a modest standard of comfort, this would imply an increase of combined GNP today of more than $1,000 billion. No foreigners are going to put up even a small fraction of this sum now or over the next generation. Therefore, rates of economic growth for poor countries will be primarily determined by domestic efforts, not by foreign assistance however great its catalytic role may be.

THE ROLE OF TRADE AND INVESTMENT

Because it is new and dramatic, foreign aid is much discussed as an element of international economic policy. For this reason and also be-

[3] See particularly John D. Montgomery, *Foreign Aid in International Politics* (Englewood Cliffs, N.J.: Prentice-Hall, 1967).

cause it looms large in international diplomacy, it sometimes seems to overshadow the role of trade in the relations between rich and poor countries (sometimes called *North-South trade*). But the value of this trade is far larger than the aid flows; in 1968, the South's exports totalled $43 billion, of which 80 per cent went to the North.[4]

Economic theory as traditionally advanced leads to the conclusion that, under competitive conditions, trade and foreign investment are likely to promote the economic development of poor countries. Trade provides a market for primary commodities, the food and raw material exports of poor countries, in which their international competitive position is strong. As the developed countries deplete their material resources, they become increasingly dependent on underdeveloped countries' commodity exports. The export revenues can be used in part to finance the imports of capital equipment needed to increase productivity in agriculture and industry. With the passage of time, the steady growth of foreign demand for primary products, and the growth of domestic industry according to comparative advantage, the developing countries become "developed."

International trade also plays another role in domestic industrialization, as competitive pressures from the world market tend to force down domestic prices and costs in the South, which ensures that domestic resources are not devoted to production by high-cost industries. Foreign private investment will tend to flow into developing areas so long as capital shortages there lead to higher rates of return than the investor can secure at home. The net effect of trade and investment is, then, to accelerate substantially the rate at which developing countries can grow by providing additional resources through trade and by the stimulus of the world market to the domestic economy.

This so-called "neoclassical" view of trade is forcefully expressed by Professor Gottfried Haberler and is representative of the views of many economists. But there is also a substantial body of dissent from this view. The selections by Gunnar Myrdal and Raúl Prebisch present another outlook. They see the international economy as operating in some ways against the interests of the poor countries. For Prebisch, the major problem is a tendency for the terms of trade (average export prices divided by average import prices) to turn against producers of primary products (which account for almost 90 per cent of less-developed countries' export earnings). This would mean that developing countries could produce and export ever-larger quantities without increasing the value of

[4] Only $1.5 billion of this total went to Communist countries, which play a small but increasing role in North-South trade.

their revenues. There is some empirical evidence to support this argument, but the majority of economists remain unconvinced.

The value of poor countries' exports has increased only about half as fast as that of industrial countries in recent years, and chronic balance-of-payments problems, operating as a brake on imports and economic growth, are commonplace in underdeveloped countries. Those adhering to the neoclassical view tend to view the payments crises as a consequence of overvalued currencies, to be cured by devaluation. Prebisch and Myrdal view these crises as a necessary consequence of the operations of the world economy, to be cured only through major policy changes discussed below.

Myrdal also feels that the effects of international commerce may be harmful to poor countries' growth because they set up a "demonstration effect" leading people in poor countries to imitate the consumption standards of rich countries. The result, according to Myrdal, is a reduction of savings and investment, which means slower growth of income and a perpetuation of poverty and discontent.

Although there is no consensus on these issues, most international economists today seem to take a position midway between the neoclassical and structural views. For example, an international conference of economists, convening shortly before the first United Nations Conference on Trade and Development (UNCTAD), advanced an agreed statement on the principal issues of world trade policy, taking rich countries to task for excessive protectionism and LDCs for high-cost industrial development and for insufficient economic cooperation with other countries.[5] This critique is consistent with neoclassical views, but some of their policy recommendations, such as partial espousal of preferential tariff treatment for underdeveloped countries in rich countries' markets, are departures from the traditional view.

INTERNATIONAL ECONOMIC POLICY TODAY: THE UNCTAD ISSUES

The debate over appropriate theoretical constructs for international economic policies is still unresolved. But there is little doubt as to the facts of the present situation. It supports the generalization that, in the world economy today, the rich are getting richer and the poor are getting children. Per capita income in rich countries is rising by more than 3 per cent annually, compared with about 2 per cent in

[5] *New Directions for World Trade,* Proceedings of a Chatham House Conference, Oxford University Press Inc., New York, 1964.

LDCs. Rich countries' exports are growing twice as fast as poor ones'. From 1950 to 1966, world exports rose by 234 per cent, and LDC exports, by 96 per cent. During the same period, population in poor countries grew at the average rate of 2.2 per cent a year, just twice as fast as industrial countries' population.

These trade trends, summarized in the articles by Barbara Ward and Sherwood Fine, have led to insistent demands by the LDCs for a restructuring of international economic policies and institutions. Their demands have been fortified by their increasing majorities in the United Nations and its specialized agencies. More than 80 of the 119 members of the United Nations are LDCs. Though their economic and military power may be modest, their votes count in international diplomacy.

In 1963, the LDCs succeeded in passing a resolution establishing a United Nations Conference on Trade and Development, which they envisioned as an agent of their efforts to recast the world trading and financial systems. This effort was further stimulated by the LDC conviction that existing international trade institutions are oriented toward the rich countries' needs. The General Agreement on Tariffs and Trade (GATT) has operated as the focus for postwar tariff-cutting rounds culminating in substantial tariff reductions authorized in May, 1967, at the conclusion of the 4-year "Kennedy Round" negotiations.

These progressive reductions in the trade barriers that were imposed between World Wars I and II have been an important factor in the expansion of world trade since 1948. However, the GATT reductions obviously did not have equal effects on LDC trade. There were several reasons. The most important is the structure of LDC trade. Nearly ninety per cent of the poor countries' exports are primary commodities. For tropical products such as tea, cocoa, coffee, and rubber, it is slow growth of demand, not tariffs, that impede trade expansion. Products that compete with rich countries' production (grains, sugar, meat, fruits, vegetable oils, etc.) are generally excluded from GATT negotiations, a testimony to the strength of agricultural protectionism in rich countries. In addition to market restrictions resulting from tariff barriers and import prohibitions, primary commodity exporters face increasing competition from synthetics (synthetic rubber, fibers, and plastics), which also holds down the growth of exports.

Another reason for the failure of GATT rounds to help LDCs greatly is that much of the two decades' trade growth following World War II was in manufactured products. Only a handful of poor countries (such as Hong Kong, India, and Israel) are yet equipped to compete in world markets for manufactures. Most of them are still in the process of building and organizing their own domestic industry, generally behind high tariff walls. Until these industries become competitive, and in many cases the prospect is remote, they are not helped much by nondiscriminatory tariff cuts.

A third element that dims the luster of the Kennedy Round in LDC eyes is inherent in the nature of existing tariff systems. All countries, rich and poor alike, tend to impose low or zero duties on raw materials and progressively higher ones on manufactures according to the stage of processing. For example, copper ore might typically be imported at zero duty, refined copper at a 5 per cent duty, copper wire at 15 per cent, etc. The net effect of this structure is often to impose very high duties on the value added by manufacturing, as Harry Johnson's article points out. Estimates published in 1966 indicate that the rich countries' effective tariff on value added for manufactured goods is about double the published tariff rate. This escalating of tariff structure means that an underdeveloped country seeking to process its raw materials for export may find itself effectively barred from foreign markets.

Furthermore, rich countries tend to protect most highly their depressed industries, as in the case of agriculture cited above. In manufacturing, the depressed industries often include those with a high ratio of labor costs to total value. These are often the very industries in which LDCs do have some competitive potential—textiles, clothing, leather products, cutlery, and a number of other light manufactures. The high duties are often justified by the North on the grounds of unfair competition from low-wage industries, which further increases LDC suspicion of industrial countries' motives.

This suspicion was elevated to a principle in 1963 when the developed countries ratified a long-term textile agreement setting quantitative limits to their textile imports from developing countries. LDCs took this to mean that rich countries were perfectly willing to encourage trade competition among themselves but unwilling to give newcomers access to their markets for manufactured products.

The sponsors of UNCTAD viewed the new organization not simply as a forum where LDCs could work to restructure world trade policy in their interests but also as an institutional catalyst for changes in international aid, investment, and monetary policies, all of which are now defective in LDC eyes.

Aid levels are now below the target of 1 per cent of rich countries' national incomes voted by the United Nations General Assembly, and lower by a good deal if allowance is made for factors that reduce the costs to donors (such as loans at commercial rates of interest) or the value to recipients (such as the requirement that recipients spend the aid only for donors' products). Furthermore, the practice of extending aid in the form of loans rather than grants has hit some poor countries with a large annual bill for debt repayment, one that they can ill afford in view of chronic foreign exchange shortages.

Foreign private investment is the traditional source of capital inflows. But since about 1950 it has not loomed as large as foreign aid. For the period 1956 to 1965, direct Northern private investment in developing countries averaged less than $3 billion net a year (about half the current level of official aid), and showed no particular trend. Meanwhile, Northern investments in other industrial countries rose rapidly; for example, during the 1957 to 1966 period, annual United States direct investments in Europe quadrupled, while those in Latin America declined (a large decline in investment in Latin American minerals was not fully compensated for by increased United States investment in industry there). As a result of these contrasting trends, the relative value of United States capital investments in developing countries declined from one-half of total United States foreign investment in 1950 to one-third in 1965.

The predominant role of rich countries as hosts for foreign investment is not hard to explain. They are generally much more attractive markets for investment. They account for most of the world's output of goods and services and their economic systems and methods of operation are relatively similar, their economies closely integrated, their legal and political institutions stable, their domestic markets large and relatively safe for investment. In the South, domestic markets are small, governments unstable, the business environment strange, and expectations uncertain. Therefore, Northern capital moves Southward mostly for investments in petroleum and minerals, the raw materials that feed industrial society. Northern investments in domestic industry in the South are relatively small, although they have grown considerably since the 1950's. Nor are the medium-term prospects for investment increases very favorable while the political and economic situations of North and South remain so far part. The article by the White House Conference on International Cooperation deals with possible approaches to catalyzing foreign investment.

THE UNCTAD RESPONSE

The net effect of current trends in aid, trade, and private investment, therefore, is to reinforce the South's conviction that the benefits of international economic relations accrue largely to the North. UNCTAD is the South's institutional response to the problem, and Raúl Prebisch, the first Secretary-General of UNCTAD, is among its leading ideologues. His reports to the first UNCTAD sessions, reprinted in part here, offers a platform for reorganizing world economic policy. The policy elements of the platform were ratified in the recommendations of the Conference[6] and have become the pillars of organized LDC negotiations in international forums.

The basic argument of UNCTAD is that the present systems of world trade and international finance are inherently biased against the interests of undeveloped countries.

The analytical foundation for the UNCTAD thesis is based on these elements: slow growth of demand for traditional LDC exports, a tendency for terms of trade (export prices divided by import prices) to turn against LDCs as a consequence of differences in labor supply conditions and market structures between rich and poor countries, and a tendency for commercial policies in rich countries to exclude LDC exports of processed products and manufactured goods.

The combined effect of these tendencies, it is alleged, is: (1) to retard the growth of LDC export markets; (2) to create serious difficulties for their industrial development by denying them mass markets for industry abroad as a substitute for the mass markets they lack at home (domestic markets being considered inadequate because of low incomes and small LDC populations, typically, less than 10 million); (3) to deny LDCs the foreign exchange that they require as a condition of economic development.

Each of these points merits some discussion. It is indisputable that the value of LDC exports has increased slowly since 1957 and that LDC terms of trade have not been favorable since then, as compared with the mid-fifties. This by no means proves the UNCTAD thesis that the commodity prices tend to decline relative to those of manufactured goods as a consequence of monopoly conditions for labor and manufactured goods in industrial countries. An alternative hypothesis might be that supply of commodities has been growing faster than demand and demand is not very responsive to price changes in the short run.

As to the second point, there is little doubt that the existing structure of protection in developed countries—including tariff and nontariff barriers, such as the textile agreement—tends to restrict the developing countries' opportunities to export processed raw materials and manufactured goods. A reduction in trade barriers would frequently result

[6] Published as Final Act and Report, Vol. I, of the *Proceedings of the United Nations Conference on Trade and Development,* United Nations, New York, 1964.

in a shift of raw-materials processing industries back toward the materials source. Mineral ores would be refined where the mines are, oil seeds would be refined into vegetable oils in the South, etc. However, for more advanced manufactured products (consumer goods, machinery, etc.), free trade may give the competitive advantage to industrial countries rather than to those whose industry remains relatively new and inefficient. There is therefore no guarantee that nondiscriminatory access to the markets of rich countries will in fact catalyze LDC industrial growth. The effects of the Kennedy Round over its first five to ten years will cast some light on the question.

There can be no serious doubts on the truth of the third proposition, that the LDCs' growth is being retarded by foreign-exchange shortages. Again, however, there is doubt concerning the causes. In opposition to the UNCTAD view, many economists put the blame on the policies of LDCs. They suggest that the shortage results primarily from currency overvaluation and excessive protection of domestic industry, which leads to inefficient use of LDC resources. The gap between export receipts and the import requirements that are generated by a development plan could, in their eyes, readily be filled by monetary and tariff policies aimed at export promotion, instead of industrialization via import substitution.

The UNCTAD formula specifically rejects currency devaluation as a primary technique for export promotion because it would put too much of the adjustment burden on LDCs.

It proposes that the unmet foreign exchange needs of the developing countries—estimated by the United Nations at $20 billion annually by 1970—be filled by five major instruments:

1. International commodity agreements aimed at raising and stabilizing prices of traditional LDC exports. (See article by John Pincus.)
2. Preferential tariff treatment for LDC manufactured exports in Northern markets to provide temporary infant-industry advantages there for the industrial development of the South. (See article by Harry Johnson.)
3. More generous terms and conditions for foreign aid to reduce the pressure of debt service from prior and new loans. (See article by Raúl Prebisch.)
4. Establishment of an international fund, known as "supplementary finance," paid for by rich countries to advance foreign exchange to LDCs whose export receipts (and development prospects) fall below anticipated levels as a consequence of factors beyond the control of individual countries (as, for example, if a worldwide recession or development of synthetic substitutes for commodity exports reduces foreign demand for an LDC's output). (See article by Raúl Prebisch.)

5. Promotion of economic integration among LDCs (in the form of common markets, free trade areas, and similar arrangements) in order to expand their domestic markets. (See article by Sidney Dell.)

There are also a number of lesser elements in the UNCTAD platform, including: international monetary reforms aimed at creating more international purchasing power for LDCs; measures to reduce the adverse balance-of-payments effects of service transactions in banking, insurance, etc.; reduction of shipping freight rates and development of Southern merchant marines; measures to speed and cheapen the transfer of technology from rich to poor countries; liberalization of nontariff barriers to Northern imports of LDC manufactures.

These are the major items on the UNCTAD agenda of its second meeting, convened at New Delhi in February, 1968. They all stem from the proposition that a foreign exchange gap of about $20 billion annually must be met to achieve the 50 per cent growth target of the United Nations' Development Decade resolution. But it is not necessary to accept either that uncertain estimate or UNCTAD economic theories in order to support some or all of these measures. A number of them are consistent with entirely different views. For example, preferential treatment for LDC manufactures might be supported on a variety of grounds: They may turn LDC energies toward the world market and away from production of high-cost import substitutes for the domestic market. They may offer to Northern private capital the motives for investing more in the South, with the accompanying advantages stemming from modern technology, training of workers and managers, improved marketing systems, etc. They may offer one avenue to economic efficiency in raw-materials processing by giving investors extra incentives to build processing plants near the raw materials source.

As another example, the North might want to endorse more generous foreign-aid terms, not from any desire to fill an uncertainly defined trade gap, but simply because the mounting burden of debt-service payments in some LDCs may lead to defaults that could bring political embarrassment to the North.

On the other hand, those who are eager to promote the economic welfare of the South might find the UNCTAD proposals objectionable on a variety of grounds: Preferences could be seized on by protectionist elements in the North as a device for *de facto* restriction of imports. Commodity agreements aimed at raising prices may prove impossible to police and, even if effective, could result in substitution of synthetics or other natural products for the controlled commodity. Supplementary finance (paying LDCs the difference between actual export earnings and some target level) would offer LDCs incentives to overestimate targets, to cheat by understating exports, and to divert production into domestic channels instead of exports (because the smaller the level of exports, the larger would be the supplementary payments). The economic integration of LDCs may be considered objectionable on the grounds that areas such as Latin America and East Africa are economically complementary to North America and Europe. Therefore, substantial capital expenditures in pursuit of LDC economic integration might better be spent in pursuit of world markets.

We do not know enough about economic policy and its consequences to predict accurately the effects of the UNCTAD policies if adopted (although the articles by Johnson and Pincus contain some estimates). A few things are obvious. First, for LDCs, preferences are better than trade liberalization if the preferences are not used by the North to introduce new trade restrictions. Second, the scope of price-fixing commodity agreements is probably limited to a few products (coffee, cocoa, tea, sugar, and tin) produced primarily by LDCs and facing little competition from substitutes produced in rich countries. Of course, price fixing is not the only way to improve the lot of commodity producers in underdeveloped countries. Subsidy systems, which do not affect world prices directly, could be applied to many products. However, governments of rich and poor countries alike have generally been reluctant to help farmers by direct subsidy; price-fixing arrangements give the illusion to farmer and legislator alike that the resulting income transfer is determined by the market rather than by political whim.

Third, supplementary finance—the UNCTAD proposal aimed at compensating countries whose export proceeds fall below some agreed target through factors beyond the exporter's control—does not offer LDCs enough incentive to adapt their economic policies to donors' criteria. The levels of supplementary finance payments from rich to poor countries currently being discussed amount to only $300 to $400 million annually worldwide compared with a 1966 foreign-aid total of about $7.4 billion. It is not certain that this sum would be in addition to existing aid. It might simply change the forms of aid without affecting the total.

Fourth, the prospects for LDC economic integration are unclear. On the one hand, most LDCs are so small and so poor that they cannot develop a range of low-cost domestic industries. If markets can be expanded by economic integration, the possibilities for industrialization are increased. (This is similar to the argument for preferences.) On the other hand, if integration simply leads to reserving LDC markets for each other's high-cost protected industry as a substitute for low-cost products from the North, then everyone is worse off. Some LDC efforts at economic integration, notably the Central American Common Market, have appeared to be quite successful. Other attempts, including East Africa's and the record to date of the Latin American Free Trade Area, are less impressive. There is evidence in the Latin American case that economic nationalism is stronger than the political will to unite.

At the first UNCTAD meetings in 1964, the North in essence rejected the LDC program. The United States was particularly adamant and voted against any commitments to the major innovations proposed, except for a few generalized expressions of good will and agreements to study the issues. The principal carrot offered by the North was the prospect of trade expansion resulting from the Kennedy Round. However large these effects may be, they are hardly calculated to satisfy the aspirations of nations convinced that the trading system which engendered the Kennedy Round is rigged against their interests. This conviction is fortified by the fact that, in the Kennedy Round, Northern tariffs on a number of products of special export interest to the South were either retained or cut by less than the average.

On the eve of the 1968 UNCTAD conference at New Delhi, the Northern position seemed to be inclining toward adoption of some elements of the LDC platform. At the Western Hemisphere conference of heads of state in April, 1967, President Johnson said that the United States was willing to consider trade preferences for all LDCs. He also endorsed United States contributions toward a fund for promoting Latin American economic integration and gave further support to the principle of international commodity agreements. However, no major concrete results, except a generalized commitment to preferences, emerged from the debating-society atmosphere of the New Delhi conference.

It remains to be seen whether these initiatives will take concrete shape and what effect they will have on the international economy. It is clear that economic policy contains no miracles. Nothing can transform the poverty and economic backwardness of Africa and Asia into an instant affluence. Even if such devices as preferences, commodity price fixing, more generous aid, stimuli to foreign investment, and economic integration are all adopted and prove effective, the economic transformation of the South remains, for most developing countries, a secular task to be accomplished largely by the LDCs' own efforts.

Each underdeveloped country, like each rich one, is different—in population, wealth, natural resources, social system, education, and every other dimension. Therefore, there is no set of international economic policies that can be equitable to all parties in the sense of offering equal benefits to each nation or individual. For example, preferences for manufactured products are sure to benefit most the relatively industrialized nations of the South such as India, Mexico, and Brazil, and impose the greatest "costs" on high-tariff importing countries. A commodity agreement for cocoa cannot help tin producers and is paid for mostly by countries whose people like sweets (Germany, Austria, and the United Kingdom). Reducing interest rates on outstanding official loans to zero helps most the big debtor nations (such as India, Argentina, and Brazil) and least those countries that have followed frugal borrowing policies. By the same token, in financial terms, such a policy costs those countries the most that have loaned large amounts at high interest rates and costs those the least who have offered their aid primarily in the form of grants.

This means that every change in international economic policies is sure to gore someone's ox. In an atmosphere of international negotiation, the only practical solution toward an objective of revising the world trading system, is to adopt a variety of policy changes so that each party feels that his interests have been considered and no one feels that he is paying excessive costs compared with others. This, in effect, is why collective bargaining—as, for example, between labor unions and management or in international tariff negotiations—frequently results in agreement. Negotiations are simultaneously carried out on a number of issues, so that each party can be made to feel that a "loss" on one point is compensated by a "gain" on another.

UNCTAD offers a forum where such simultaneous negotiations are possible. Whether it is desirable is another matter. But it is clearly far more feasible now than before the first UNCTAD. The United States has long advocated a liberal trade policy, one that discriminates in favor of no one. Yet, since 1948, it has approved many departures from the principle of nondiscrimination: the European Common Market, the European Free Trade Association, and the Central American and Latin American Common Markets. Therefore, the principle of general discrimination in favor of LDCs seems less alien to United States policy today than in the past.

European countries with their colonial traditions are accustomed to preferential economic relations, which have been sustained by the new European trade blocs. Among the major trading nations outside the Western Hemisphere, only Japan finds itself without an existing preferential framework, and Japan is also likely to pay the highest price in foreign markets as a consequence of preferential concessions to LDCs. However, Japan is not in a strong position to stand out alone against LDC policy demands because nearly half of Japan's exports go to the South.

While the temper of policy makers is clearly moving toward a mood more favorable to trade concessions, there seems to be little prospect of large-scale aid increases, despite the general view of economists, shared by many political figures and by such experts as the President of the World Bank, that LDCs could effectively use much more aid than they now receive. In fact, one principal lubricant of trade concessions is official reluctance to raise the ante for aid.

Trade concessions thus seem more feasible now than large-scale aid increases. Are they preferable? The answer involves two extensions of the question: (1) preferable for whom? (2) preferable to what other alternatives? For the rich countries, it is preferable to make the fewest possible concessions; for the poor, to negotiate the most. For the world as a whole, there is no general answer. All answers depend on what vision of international society you perceive. If the objective is to help poor countries, then both aid and trade concessions are desirable. If it is to use world resources efficiently, then competitive markets, free trade, and unrestricted private investment are the traditional economic prescriptions whose value to LDCs remains untested.

But, in practice, we do not face an unrestricted field of alternatives. World free trade and competitive markets with their uncertain effects are not an immediate prospect, nor is a vast outpouring of Northern concessions to the South. By the same token, North and South are sentenced to share the tenancy of earth, so that the North does not in practice face the alternative of wholly ignoring Southern demands. Therefore, the UNCTAD proposals must be viewed for what they are: tentative gropings by the fragmented world community to reach some agreement on mutually acceptable changes in the policies that shape the world economy. Like all such negotiations, they will satisfy no one fully because they operate in the realm of the possible, far removed from that Xanadu where the clash of material interests could be dissipated to suit the infinite diversity of men's dreams.

PART I

Rich and Poor Nations: The Problem in Its Setting

THE DECADE OF DEVELOPMENT— A STUDY IN FRUSTRATION?

Barbara Ward

Barbara Ward (Lady Jackson), Professor at Columbia University, a distinguished writer on international affairs, has long had a particular interest in the problems of the relations between rich and poor countries. For many years on the staff of the London Economist, *she has recently been a Visiting Scholar at Harvard University and a Carnegie Corporation Fellow. She is the author of a number of books, including* Policy for the West *(1951);* India and the West *(1961) and* The Rich Nations and the Poor Nations *(1962). In this article, written in 1966, she stresses the widening gap between rich and poor countries' income levels, and goes on to analyze the factors that account for the current trends.*

When I proposed the title for this lecture, I did mean there to be a question mark after "frustration"—that typical way of hedging one's bets. The statement "A Study in Frustration" is a little too strong, because, in fact, looking back over these five years of the Decade, I would say that one of the remarkable points is the number of things that we have learnt about the processes of development. These could in turn be the springboard for better action in the rest of the Decade. So, if you do not mind, I am going to put that query back, and I hope that I shall be able to show you why.

The 'fifties were the time when the whole process of development came to be seen as a world-wide pattern in which the already developed countries formed a wealthy, fully modernised "North" and the developing

Barbara Ward, "The Decade of Development," in *Two Views of Foreign Aid* (London: The Institute of Economic Affairs Ltd., 1966). Reprinted by permission of Overseas Development Institute Ltd.

continents formed the aspiring, underdeveloped, uncertain "South". And this contrast quickly entered the language of cliche. In fact, I am not sure that one of the great problems that those of us who are trying to deal with explanation and communication may not be that we over-communicate; we communicate like mad; we communicate so much that, in a very short time, the ideas that were fresh when we thought them up do not sound fresh any more. People get the idea that something has been done about a problem because it is constantly being talked about. And I fear that, with the Decade of Development, the sheer force of repetition is making it difficult to get a freshness of approach, and therefore a freshness of attack, in this field. So if I appear to begin with some of the cliches, try to think of them not as cliches, but as truisms; then remind yourselves, with Chesterton, that truisms are also true.

In the 'fifties, then, we got used to the concept of a "North" and a "South". The whole idea of a Decade of Development lay in the belief that we could so hasten up development in the "South" of our planet that, in fact, ten years could be taken as a meaningful period for basic change. This was our first reaction to the discovery of the disparities between "North" and "South", the discovery that in a world which was modernising itself as a whole planetary society, some parts of it were modernising or had modernised themselves very much more rapidly than the rest.

No doubt all of you will recall what are the general targets of the Decade of Development. They are that the 3½ per cent annual rate of growth in gross national product—quite a respectable rate of growth—achieved by the "Southern" developing countries in the 'fifties should be brought up to a 5 per cent rate of growth, and that, if possible, it should be pushed up towards 6 per cent at the end of the Decade. In addition, it was hoped that the share of the developing countries in world trade would go up from 26 to 28 per cent—rather a modest little target which gives the developing countries no more than the share they enjoyed at the beginning of the 1950s. It was also hoped that the terms of trade, which, after the end of the post-Korean war boom, had moved rather sharply against the primary producing countries, might move back, if not by the whole 12 lost points, then at least by eight. Last of all, it was hoped that the developed countries, to be defined by some criterion of national income, say $700 *per capita,* would aim by the middle of the Decade of Development to be giving 1 per cent of their national income in economic assistance. Such aid would be recognisable as genuine assistance. For example, it would not consist of commercial loans for five years at 8 per cent—which have an uncomfortable way of creeping into aid when no one is looking.

WIDENING GAP

These, broadly speaking, were the targets of the decade. One important point to be made from the outset is their equal emphasis upon aid *and* trade. The uneven balance in the world economy between the wealthy group largely in the North, with *per capita* incomes of $700 and more, and the rest of the developing world with national incomes *per capita* of $200 and less, cannot be set right simply by transfers of skills, resources and investment. There is also an extremely urgent problem of imbalance in international trade, one masked by the consequences first of the war and then of the post-Korean war boom, but which by the end of the 1950s was beginning to emerge as one of the basic causes of uneven development.

Such were the aims five years ago. Let us begin by trying to see where we are now, half way through the Decade. In some ways, it has not gone too badly. But the reason is that it has gone *so* well for the developed countries that their success has been 'trickle-down' or residual effects on the developers. Yet at the end of the five years, the gap between rich nations and poor is greater still, not because the poor have necessarily grown poorer, but because the rich have got richer by so much more. This disproportion can be measured in a number of ways. For instance, most of the developed countries, to be found in the main round the North Atlantic, have got back to rates of growth of about 5 to 6 per cent a year, or rather they have either maintained them, as in Europe, or got back to them, as in the United States. This has meant, on top of their original wealth, a surge forward in the whole level of their economy. To give you only one example, in 1964 the United States *added* to its national income the equivalent of the entire national income of the African continent—some 30,000 million dollars. This shows the sort of built-in accelerating process which growth on top of wealth implies.

In trade, the terms of trade have moved back a little in favour of the primary producers, but in a very uneven way. If you are in the minerals business, you have done very nicely. If you are in natural fibres, you have continued to do miserably. If you are in temperate food, the position is not very good, unless, of course, you are a protected Western farmer. Tropical products go up and down in the usual way. But cocoa faces a really desperate crisis with prices lower than at any time since the great slump of the 'thirties. In other words, there has been an overall recovery in the terms of trade of primary producers of about eight points. But if your particular commodity has not been in the favourable bracket, then you are no better off and possibly worse off than you were at the end of the 1950s.

The relative shares in world trade have not improved. This is not because the trade of the developing world has not been going up. It has. But the share of the developed countries and their trade with each other—which, after all, makes up over 70 per cent of world trade —has increased even more. In fact, in this whole picture, the old biblical phrase that "to him who hath shall be given"—which, of course, is the law of unredeemed economics—has been working with perfect clarity and precision over the last five years.

This pattern of change has its impact upon economic assistance. It is not that the rich are giving less. At the beginning of the 'sixties their capital transfers moved up quite sharply to seven to eight billion dollars a year (though this figure does include some rather more dubious and "commercial" forms of aid). But since that increase, assistance has stayed on a plateau. During the same period, however, the rich have been getting very much richer. Therefore, proportionately to national income, their assistance has begun to fall. Nearly all the developed countries now, with the exception of France, give well below 1 per cent of national income, and this percentage, at the moment, is tending to fall further. So once more we see the phenomenon, not of an absolute fall, but of a relative change in favour of the richer countries. That, I think, sums up where we are today—not a disastrous deterioration, indeed, quite a few grounds for hope. But nearly all of it is "trickle-down" hope, the by-product of the fact that the rich countries have been doing very well indeed. The vast majority of mankind in over 100 developing countries are roughly where they were before—with rates of increase in *per capita* income of 2 per cent a year and less. If one excludes the five or six nations—such as Greece or Taiwan or Israel—which are growing at phenomenal rates of over 7 per cent *per capita* a year—the world in the mid-'sixties has made no progress in lessening the "North-South" gap.

CAUTION NOT PESSIMISM

When we ask why the developing countries have, on the whole, failed to share in the upward *élan* of the wealthier states, we begin, I think, to reach the new thinking of the 'sixties. It consists of a much more judicious estimate of the difficulties in the way of development. The old optimism of "development in a decade" is giving way to a wiser sense of "development in half a century". The obstacles are better defined, the strategies for overcoming them more rational.

But before we define the problems more precisely, I would like to say a word about the psychological background against which we tend to discuss the issues of development. We have perhaps been a little misled by some of our own—I will not say "jargon" because that is too strong a word—but our own "shorthand" in talking about development. We have coined such phrases as "break-through" and "take-off" and so forth, and we have an idea, I think, of economies all "hastening onwards to felicity"—as Miss Jane Austen might have put it—and have forgotten how long, how devious, how difficult the process can be. Economies do not only go forward. They go backward. They remain stationary. Developed economies have often appeared to come to thresholds of decision, of choice, of change of direction, yet have in fact repeatedly muffed the chance. If we look back over the history of fully developed economies such as the British economy or that of the United States, we can choose a number of past decades during which we would have hesitated to call them "dynamic" at all. The 'twenties and the 'thirties are a good enough example of my point. The whole concept of dynamic growth as being the *normal* state of an economy is relatively new and something about which we still, in spite of our "shorthand", do not know too much. When I was growing up and first learning about economics, the North Atlantic economies—it was in the 'thirties—were going through what one can perhaps call a very constipated patch. We were not taught "growth" economics because so little growth was observable around us. Our theories of dynamism today spring from the fact that, once more, since the war our economies have apparently got back into the habits of growth.

But it is quite possible that the theories we derive from the behaviour of our well-established economies do not apply too handily to infant economies struggling in the first stages of change. We have a lot to learn and this fact should teach us a certain caution in our assessment of where, at any precise moment, an economy has arrived in the matter of dynamism or momentum. But this is not a wholly pessimistic point. There is also matter here for optimism. In the big penumbra of still under-developed economies, we cannot be absolutely certain at which point a phase of acceleration may not set in. We cannot predict it will start. But equally we need not be discouraged by any certainty that it will not. To give you one example, it seems to me that, quite apart from the vagaries of monsoon weather, agriculture in Pakistan is beginning to show new dynamic features. The last big period of growth came half a century ago with the tremendous structural changes of irrigation in the Punjab. But since the war, the farm situation has been more or less static and has even deteriorated in some places because of salinisation. But over the last five years a new and decisive breakthrough appears to be taking place. Tube wells, which provide enough water to make the use of fertiliser profitable, subsidies for both wells and fertiliser, a far greater emphasis on marketing—these are elements in a policy which seems to have raised the rate of growth in agriculture from the 1 per cent of the 'fifties—which left the food supply below the scale of population growth—to about 3.5 per cent which begins to put Pakistan ahead of it. Thus I think Pakistan may well be an interesting example of my argument—that we never can be absolutely sure at which point previous inputs of capital and previous developments of trained personnel may not, through some alchemy of circumstances, begin to produce the sort of dynamism that makes "take-off" possible.

The present fact of relative stagnation in the developing world and the relative lack of progress over the last five years must not, therefore, be taken to mean that dynamism will be indefinitely delayed and that the "South" can never, for a variety of often discreditable reasons, hope to catch up. The moment at which momentum begins to take hold and become a habit was unpredictable in the "North". So it is in the "South". There is no cause for discouragement. But there *is* need for much more analysis, for more well-designed strategies and for very much more determination. It must be our hope that the 'sixties are bringing all three.

NEED FOR MORE ANALYSIS

First, then—analysis. What are the blocks to more rapid development? The first I want to pick out lies in the political fact of colonial and semi-colonial dependence. Most of the "Southern" economies were first introduced to modernisation by the Western industrial countries. But the process did not leave them strictly in command of their own economies and in the first decades of the new impact they were not in the position to take a number of decisions which could, at various points, have changed the pattern and quality of their economic life.

They had been stimulated to the beginnings of economic growth by the need of the industrial powers of the North Atlantic for raw materials, for tropical products and, up to a point, for temperate food supplies. Western investment went to the other continents to open up mines, farms and plantations and Western trade organised the international markets needed to exchange "Southern" primary products for "Northern" manufactures. The resulting pattern was one of a very strong development of the local import/export sector but there followed very little "spread effect" from this sector to the rest of the economy. The transactions did not naturally generate much local credit because they remained something of a closed circuit largely under foreign control. The raw materials were sent out to pay for the original investment. Profits, capital gains and sometimes a ten-fold amortisation returned to the metropolitan investors. What local purchasing power was generated was mopped up by the sale of Western manufactures imported through large Western trading companies. Since the process did not stimulate much credit locally, little capital was available for investment in the modernisation of food-producing agriculture. It is typical of Asia, Africa and Latin America that the old forms of agriculture have persisted largely unchanged, outside the plantations and—in a few areas—the peasants' cash crops. Nor was capital available for local industry. There were few local entrepreneurs and, in any case, the satisfaction of the market with Western manufactures was part of the essential pattern.

In this situation only strong, direct governmental intervention would have modified the situation. On the one hand, it could have transformed the agricultural scene. The peasant/landlord relationship could have been changed in Asia, freehold introduced into the communal tribal agriculture of Africa, the *latifundia* abolished in Latin America. On the other, industry could have been stimulated by governmental decisions in the field of mobilising savings and of building up protective tariffs behind which local enterprise could have started to grow. But these were precisely the kind of decisions which are not ordinarily taken by colonial governments. Part of the reason was their traditional philosophy of *laissez faire*. Part lay in the fact that it was not in the interest of their own trading and investing circles. Even where governments were not directly colonial—as in Latin America—the small ruling groups preferred to work with the foreign investors for limited personal gains rather than risk general reforms in the economy—one reason for Latin America's long economic stagnation. All through the colonial and semi-colonial world, the century since the 1850s has seen a fair amount of economic stimulus and development. But since the continents lacked either the governmental power or the governmental will to break the bottlenecks, the barriers to a wider modernisation remained intact and growth was confined to a narrow sector.

These inhibitions can be clearly seen in the striking contrast between India and Japan. In colonial India there was, in fact, a certain amount of industrial development, particularly where entrepreneurial talent was locally strong, as it was in and around Bombay. But if we compare the relative snail's pace of Indian industrial growth between 1870 and 1920 with the forced draft industrialisation of Japan over the same period, it can be seen, I think, that India chiefly lacked an apparatus of political decision for breaking the deadlocks which the process of growth does not overcome of itself. In Japan, a root and branch land reform, the compensation of landlords in government bonds which could only be invested in new government-established industries, the mobilisation of credit in country and town, the drive to literacy, government sponsorship of overseas training—in short, an entire battery of development strategies was carried out by a vigorous and resourceful government. In India, there was no sponsorship of industry, land reform was not touched—in spite of the increasing debt of the peasants—no particular push for general education occurred and the Indian government could not even impose a tariff until 1920. It was in fact only after 1947, with the establishment of full, independent, decision-making machinery, that India began to tackle economic problems Japan had been dealing with since the 1870s.

It does not, of course, always follow that when the local government does get the power to make its own economic decisions, it makes only the right ones. My point is that, practically speaking, up to the very end of the colonial period, local leaders were in no position to make any decisions at all. Yet in any process of development there has to be a decision-making power to deal with blocks and barriers which the sheer momentum of the economic process itself does not overcome.

POPULATION CONTRADICTIONS

Another whole range of structural difficulties has arisen from the time sequences of development—from the timing of inventions and changes, the order in which they appeared and the differing consequences of different sequences of cause and effect. These are not easy for us to grasp in the West for we know our own history best and tend to generalise from our own experience. But just because we were the pioneers, we missed many contradictions which were simply not present in the early phases of development among the industrial nations of the North Atlantic. I do not need to underline the most obvious contradiction. It is the best-known and perhaps the most discussed. But it must at least be mentioned. Even with the fairly moderate health measures which are available in the developing world today, life expectancy has been about doubled. In fact, if we wanted to pick on one of the real achievements of the last 20 years in the developing world, we would point out that the expectation of life has lengthened from 25 years to 45 years.

True, it is still 20 years behind the life expectancy in the developed world. But a 20-year lengthening of life coupled with traditional rates of fertility and rather less infantile mortality has sent the population growth spurting ahead of any possible modernisation of the economy. This is the situation throughout the developing world. Since 1960, at least a score of censuses have been held, under United Nations auspices, in developing countries, in nine of them for the first time. I believe I am right in saying that in every state—with the possible exception of Liberia—population was found to be higher than had been expected and the rates of expansion to be more rapid. Most of the estimates of population increases made towards the end of the 'fifties are now being revised upwards. In Pakistan and India it is already up to 2.8 per cent. It probably should be 2.9 per cent and by 1970 it is pretty well certain to be 3 per cent. Central America has reached the fabulous figure of 3.5 per cent already. Most of Latin America, outside Argentina, is at or moving rapidly towards the 3 per cent level. It is such figures as these that have reduced the growth in *per capita* income to almost nil in the developing world. And it is this rate of increase, produced by health measures in advance of most other forms of modernisation, that creates dilemmas for developing economies today which the Atlantic world largely avoided. There, almost without exception, the whole process of modernisation and of the accumulation of savings had passed the critical stage by the time population growth began to grow with really startling speed. In fact, in spite of Malthus's gloom about growing population pressure, many early economists in Britain argued that the new industrial system would break down because of a labour shortage. Lack of manpower would force up wages, squeeze out profits and bring investments to an end.

In the event, it seems to have worked in reverse. Growth of population, occurring *after* a breakthrough into greater mechanisation and productivity, acts as a spur to further growth. Once the apparatus of supply has been created, an increase in demand, *via* the formation of new families, acts as a steady stimulus to further expansion of the tools and machines and whole capability of the economy to satisfy yet further demand.

I think we should take notice of all this reversal of the early gloom about the rigid limits of expansion. The classical economists believed in the ineluctable tendency of costs to outpace profits, once supplies—of resources, of labour, of capital—began to become used up and scarce (in other words, at the margin). In fact, technology has increased productivity in such a startling way that, in any but the very short run, the margin recedes and recedes. Profits and wages go up together and the incentives to invest and the ability to consume, far from being contradictory, reinforce each other in the modern mass-consumption economy. Ricardo, Malthus, Nassau Senior, Mill, even Marx were all proved over-pessimistic. This is one more reason for avoiding discouragement today—and putting a question mark after the word "frustration".

But the outlook is not necessarily the same when population expands *ahead* of productivity. This is the real Malthusian trap. To introduce the full technology of modernisation—in farming and industry—requires greater saving. But longer lives and new mouths push up consumption at the expense of saving. I need not labour the point; but it is important to remember that the reversal of the time factor of the West—industry first, health later—spared the Atlantic nations this profound dilemma.

TECHNOLOGICAL DISPROPORTION

Now let us look at another problem caused by differences in timing. The technology which is dominant in the world today is not always appropriate to the needs of the developing countries—and this for a very simple reason. The whole weight of economic research and of investment in further research is virtually confined to the developed countries and has, for 50 years and more, taken the form of trying to find labour-saving methods of production. In other words, modern technology is largely designed to substitute machines for manpower. In addition, it is designed more and more for large units and for large markets. But large-scale, labour-saving technologies constitute, at this stage of development, the least suitable methods of production for continents such as Asia where the one abundant resource is labour or for countries like many African countries in which the one potentially competitive resource is labour that is still relatively cheap.

This is a disproportion which the developed world never knew since it invented and pioneered and adapted its technology to its own needs as the process of development went on. But now the technology exists in its own right and can be purchased and introduced into societies in which in fact it is quite inappropriate. One can see the consequences of this maladjustment very clearly in some parts of Africa today. Inexperienced governments, trying out their hand in economic decision-making, find it terribly tempting to buy the most up-to-date machinery which persuasive gentlemen from the North Atlantic area come to sell them. These salesmen call their efforts "investment". In fact they only offer suppliers' credits at fairly high rates of interest and at prices which tend to be far above the international level. They are, as it were, plumping down great gobbits of advanced industrial technology into countries where there is neither the market nor the skills nor the managerial capacity nor indeed any of the pre-conditions for such a technology to work successfully.

These policies constitute not only a big block in the way of development, but they do little to improve economic relations between North and South. They are bound, as in Ghana today, to precipitate a crisis in the balance of payments. For how can these suppliers' credits be repaid when they have been invested in industrial structures which have absolutely no hope of paying their way? They were not related organically to any accurate economic analysis in the first place. They were fancy goods sold from the Western shop window and they are inappropriate in technology and inappropriate as a stimulus to growth inside the economy. The factory chimneys may smoke indeed, but they are factories operating at one-third of capacity and producing goods which nobody can afford to buy locally and which do not compete on the world market. Under such conditions, a country may nominally industrialise and "develop" but in fact its standard of living actually falls.

This disproportion in technology also spills over into the field of trade. In the developed world, the use of substitutes constantly goes up because contemporary research is largely concentrated upon the products of the industrial countries. If, as a cheap byproduct of petro-chemicals, Western industry can produce a substitute, say, for binder twine which is only half the price of sisal, the consequences from the point of view of the petro-chemical interests—which are large, efficient and able to afford the research—are obviously very satisfactory. But for Tanganyika and for large parts of Kenya the elimination of sisal would mean a total disaster for their limited range of exports. I do not argue that no adjustments should be made. I simply point out that in the present world pattern of research, the adjustments are continuously having to be made by those countries which can least afford to do so, which have least economic choice and flexibility and are least able to adjust to rapid change. Thus the concentration of successful research in the developed North has its effect not only on the technology of investment, but the technology of trade as well. This is one reason why, in the whole balance of trade between the developed and the developing countries, there is a built-in tendency for some of the old 19th century advantages in the division of labour to be whittled away and the pendulum to swing against the primary producers.

PSYCHOLOGICAL CROSS-CURRENTS

Now let me speak of a disproportion of structural difficulty not so much in the technological as in the psychological field. In one sense it may not be very important that the developing South feels itself a late-comer in the new system of science and technology. Fifty years from now, the distinction will not matter since what we are witnessing is the steady transformation of the whole human race by science and technology. In the short run, however, the result of being a late-comer is that aims and ambitions tend to be determined not by local experience but by the world's vast shop window of new and desirable techniques and objects. This "demonstration effect" offered by the fully developed societies creates quite special problems for new governments. Countries which have just acquired the means of political and economic decision-making want quickly to command the whole range of opportunities which, they know, give wealth and scale and all kinds of elbow room to the already developed countries. They want to jump, in one "big leap forward", the gap between their restrictions and other nations' opportunities. Their people want it, too. This is the essence of what Adlai Stevenson used to call "the revolution of rising expectations".

A special twist to this thinking is given by the colonial experience. Nationalist leaders have tended to think that the economic basis of colonialism is sheer exploitation. The old metropolitan powers held back local development in their own interests. Abolish colonialism, so runs the argument, and the balance will be automatically redressed and full-scale modernisation achieved. The degree to which the process of development lasts over several decades and depends upon a whole range of inputs—above all, the inputs of trained minds and skills—tends to be overlooked or, when it is not forgotten, resisted and resented. Thus there exists a disproportion, a profound psychological disproportion between what governments want and what in actual fact they can quickly have. This kind of mood—which easily breeds political disaffection—was simply unknown years ago because people did not know then what other people could have. Development then was a relatively blind process in which the pioneers were only working within their own imaginative limits. But now, nations who come behind are working, if you like, within imaginative limits fixed by systems already so sophisticated, so complex, so thoroughly trained, that their range of possibility far surpasses anything that can be achieved quickly or in the short run by inexperienced societies. "Between the dream and the reality falls the shadow"—and it is a shadow of disappointment and frustration and potential political unrest.

These, then, are some of the built-in difficulties which exist not because governments in the developing South are less responsible, efficient, realistic, modest, hard-working or grateful than their critics think they should be but because they are facing the problems of modernisation in the second half of the 20th, not the 19th, century. There are, of course, other difficulties which I have not mentioned—for instance, the degree to which the earlier industrial breakthroughs, in the days before petrochemicals and nuclear energy, were based on forms of energy and on minerals which the South lacked. But the difficulties I have mentioned—colonial dependence, health before growth, inappropriate technology, unbalanced trade and over-stimulated ambitions—are quite enough to explain the Southern "lag" without resorting to cultural or—God forbid—racial criticisms.

ECONOMIC GROWTH IN THE LESS DEVELOPED COUNTRIES

Sherwood M. Fine

The Organization for Economic Cooperation and Development (OECD), established in 1961, numbers among its members the economically advanced nations of the world—North America, Western Europe and Japan. Its Development Assistance Committee deals particularly with rich countries' aid to less developed areas. Mr. Fine, a former Director in the OECD Development Department, describes the current economic situations of rich and poor countries, and some of the major outstanding policy issues affecting the economic growth of less developed countries.

GROWTH RATES

Despite the increasing efforts by the industrialised nations to step up the economic development process in the low-income countries, and their efforts on their own behalf, the income gap between these two groups is steadily widening. In 1965 per capita GNP for the 588 million inhabitants of the more-developed OECD Member countries amounted to an average of $2,220. This contrasts with an estimated average figure of some $190 per capita for the approximate 1.6 billion inhabitants of the noncommunist less-developed world. While these figures are of themselves interesting, it would be inappropriate to attribute any particular significance to them (see below for a fuller discussion) because of such factors as national differences in patterns of production and consumption, the difficulties of converting local currency income figures into dollars, and variations in price levels.

In the more-developed OECD countries, projected growth rates of real product (4.5 per cent) after allowing for a population increase of

Sherwood Fine, "Economic Growth in the Less Developed Countries," *OECD Observer,* September, 1966, pp. 23-34. Reprinted by permission of the *OECD Observer.*

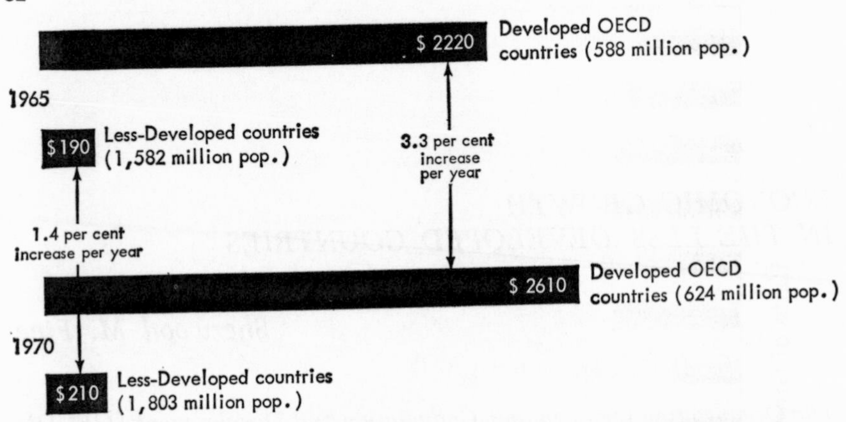

Forecasted Growth of Real Product Per Capita (At Constant 1965 Prices) [Art Redrawn]

1.2 per cent produce an average increase in per capita incomes of some $70 per annum calculated in 1964 prices. Growth is estimated as progressing at only a slightly lower rate (some 4 per cent per annum) in the less-developed countries. But the resulting increase in per capita income is only about $3 per annum after adjustment for a 2.6 per cent annual rate of population growth. Thus, measured in terms of absolute income, the more-developed nations, due to their greater income base, are advancing by annual increments to their income more than 20 times greater than those of the less-developed countries.

Considerable differences exist, of course, in the relative success achieved by individual less-developed nations in pursuing growth objectives. For example, compared with an average GNP growth rate for the less-developed world of about 4 per cent for the years 1960-65, Israel achieved a rate of 10.7 per cent, Greece 8.7 per cent, Republic of China (Taiwan) 7.4 per cent, Yugoslavia 7.0 per cent, and Mexico 6.3 per cent. Below the average are Argentina with 2.8 per cent, and Ceylon, Morocco and Paraguay experiencing growth rates between 3 and 4 per cent. India, the most populous of the less-developed countries—with a population greater than that of Africa and South America combined—had a growth rate of 2.9 per cent.

EFFECTS OF POPULATION INCREASES

The gains resulting from any given rate of increase in GNP may be largely offset by a high rate of population growth. While it is true

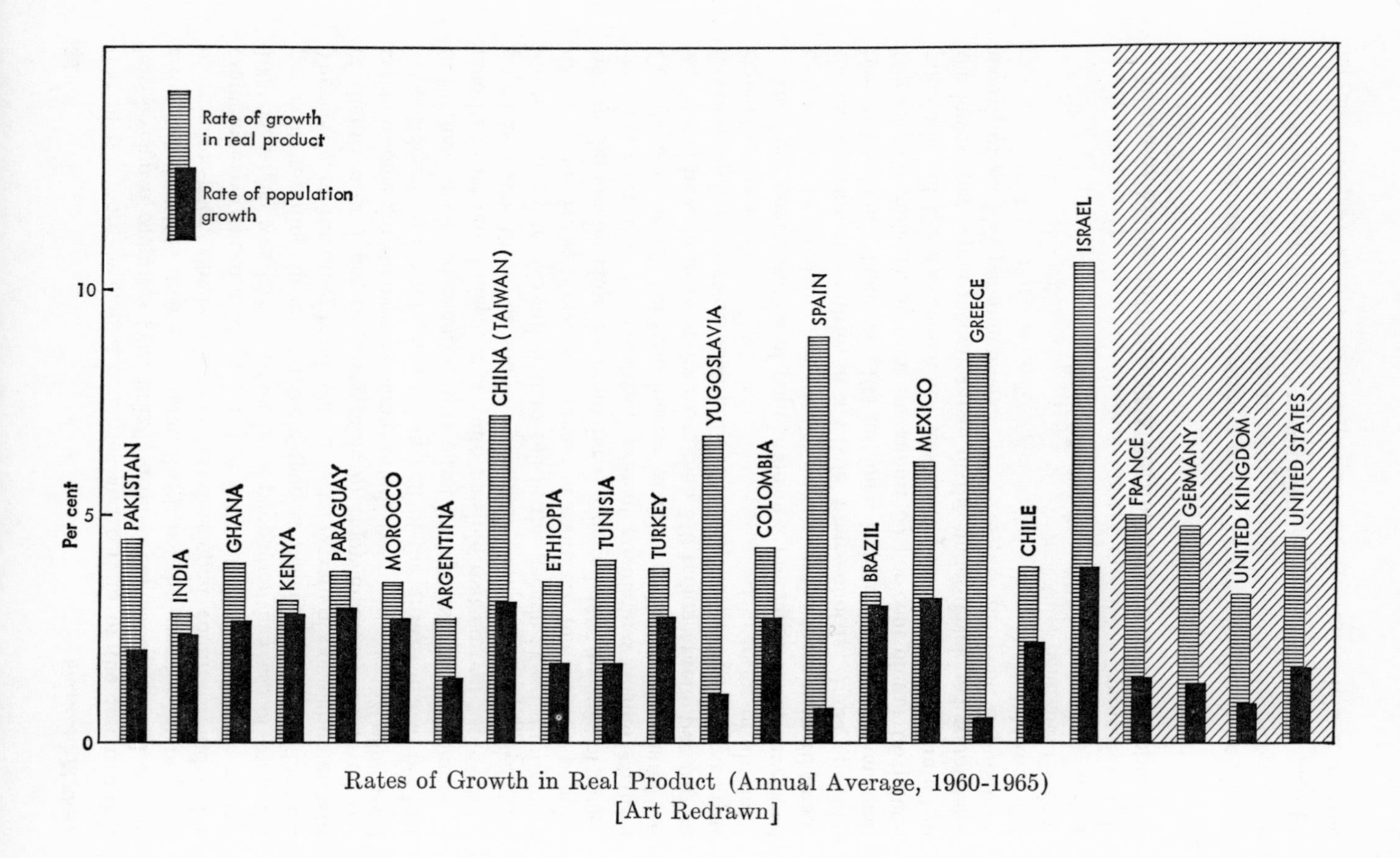

Rates of Growth in Real Product (Annual Average, 1960-1965)
[Art Redrawn]

that in the more-developed countries and certain of the resource-rich less-developed countries (viz. Brazil) a rapid population growth can be a dynamic factor in their economies, this is not the case for the majority of resource-poor, slowly adapting less-developed countries. India, for example, experienced a 2.9 per cent growth rate in GNP for the period 1960-65, which was largely offset by a population increase of some 2.4 per cent, resulting in an extremely modest rise in per capita income. Yugoslavia, on the other hand, with a very low rate of population growth of slightly over 1 per cent, was able to enjoy markedly improved per capita income growth over the same period.

Considered as a whole, more than half of the growth in real product in the less-developed countries was offset by increases in the number of mouths to be fed. Indeed, it is quite possible that current estimates of population growth are on the low side and that, beyond this, the rates are more likely to rise rather than fall in the decade ahead. Profoundly disconcerting is the projected increase of some 220 million new population in the less-developed nations for the period 1965 to 1970. This increase is more than the combined present populations of the U.S. and Canada, and means that total income of the less-developed parts of the world will have to increase by more than $40 billion (present aggregate incomes amount to some $300 billion) merely to maintain current per capita income levels.

The huge concentration of population in a few large under-developed countries understandably has a major impact on the income averages for the less-developed countries as a whole. Four countries, India (population 483 million), Pakistan (103 million), Indonesia (102 million) and Nigeria (56 million), account for almost 50 per cent of the 1.6 billion population of the non-communist less-developed world. They are all in the lowest per capita income range of the under-developed countries—namely under $100 per annum.

* * *

DIFFERENCES AMONG THE LESS-DEVELOPED COUNTRIES

Despite the common denominator of low income and the preponderant importance of agriculture both in terms of employment and income, the less-developed nations differ very considerably from each other.

Natural Resources

Very great differences exist in the quality of available natural resources among the less-developed countries. Some countries such as Brazil, Chile, Indonesia and Nigeria have very great untapped resources including vast agricultural and mineral potential. Others are acutely short of arable land —Greece, Egypt, Iran and India. Of greater importance than availability of arable land is the level of agricultural technology practised. This not only varies considerably among countries for the major crops, but also within the countries taken individually. Great increases in output would become possible if the low average level of farming proficiency could be brought up to the more efficient and skilled levels occasionally practised in the individual less-developed countries.

The pattern of agriculture among the less-developed countries remains preponderantly that of subsistence farming, characterised by low output of often poorly selected crops, directed to meet the limited consumption needs of the farm family. This structure may sometimes be relieved by "islands" of efficient commercial farming concentrating on the production of crops specifically for the export market. Improvements in farm organisation and technology should supplant this dominant subsistence pattern by the progressive introduction of carefully selected cash crops produced—either for domestic or foreign consumption.

Capital Formation

The inescapable corollary of low income levels is the limited availability of domestic savings to apply to the process of capital formation. While available data on savings and gross capital investment for the less-developed world are less than satisfactory, some brief aggregate treatment may nonetheless be useful and pertinent. Considered as a whole, the underdeveloped world has had during recent years a rate of gross capital formation of somewhat more than 15 per cent of GNP. In absolute terms, this figure was roughly $45 billion for 1965. A considerable range of variations in gross capital formation is apparent among the various countries. For example, over the five-year period 1960-64, countries with highest annual rates of gross capital formation included Israel 32 per cent, Argentina and Peru 22 per cent, Venezuela, Colombia and China (Taiwan) 20 per cent. In the lower range were India, Korea (South) and Chile, each with 14 per cent.

There is, however, no precise correlation between the rate of capital formation and GNP levels. The contributory factors accounting for the variable experience are highly complex and relate to such considerations as savings and spending habits, governmental economic policy, the particular stage of economic development, etc.

Technical Skills

Pronounced variations exist in the level of technical skills and the availability of technicians. Comparatively well off are Israel, Spain, Taiwan, Yugoslavia, Mexico and Chile. Less well off are Laos, Congo, Iran, India and Pakistan. There are also great differences in the degree of effectiveness with which the available technicians are used. The vital factor of technical skills is discussed at further length later in this article.

Education

Educational facilities are generally poor at all levels, from low-level vocational and technical training to special courses for middle-level manpower as well as the gamut of general education up to the university level. Literacy rates are correspondingly low on average (roughly some 30 per cent), but perhaps far more significant are the low levels of training in technical skills immediately relevant to production. Considerable differences exist among the individual less-developed countries with respect to educational levels. While definitions of literacy differ widely and it is by no means a satisfactory barometer of technical skills, it is of interest to appreciate the great variety of literacy rates. Some of the less-developed countries have literacy rates comparable to those of the industrially advanced countries (viz. Israel, Argentina, Chile and Yugoslavia) while at the other end of the scale the overwhelming mass of the population is illiterate.

Management and Administrative Skills

Virtually all the less-developed countries suffer from acute shortages of management and administrative skills in both government and private enterprise. While there are a limited number of less-developed nations with an impressive private enterprise sector (including Greece, Malaya, Hong-Kong, Israel, Mexico, Lebanon and Taiwan) in general both public and private resources are poorly managed and development possibilities frequently neglected. Unfortunately there do not appear to be any simple or speedy devices for meeting this deficiency locally. Foreign technical assistance has a real challenge in this field. If it can have any significant effect in remedying these deficiencies it would generate a very high "multiplier" effect indeed. But the field of training is fraught with many special difficulties and, unfortunately, even at best is unlikely to produce any adequate flow of skilled managers and administrators for quite a number of years.

Level of Government Administrative Performance

The level of government administrative performance is typically not particularly high. This is, of course, not surprising given the short history of many of these countries as responsible administrative units. Further, new fields such as economic development itself have suddenly emerged as major critical areas of decision and action. Here the level of performance varies considerably depending, in part, upon the administrative legacy bequeathed to the individual newly-emerging states. However, it has not followed that relatively competent bureaucracies have necessarily performed effectively in the new field of economic development. The problems of the newly-emerging states have been complicated by losses of former colonial technicians and administrators; it takes time to replace them from other sources and to build up a cadre of national experts.

FOREIGN CAPITAL FLOWS TO THE LESS-DEVELOPED WORLD

Contributing to the approximately $45 billion investment in the less-developed countries in 1965 was about $10.3 billion net official and private capital movement from the OECD countries and international organisations. Total official net contributions received by less-developed countries amounted to some $6.7 billion while net recorded private capital investment amounted to about $3.6 billion. Net official capital movement in 1965 was slightly higher than in 1964, and it showed an increase of some 70 per cent over the average for the period 1956-1959. The figures of gross investment and net official and private capital flow are not strictly comparable, but the official flow (which finances the purchase of consumption as well as investment goods) provides some rough order of magnitude of the relative importance of foreign capital flows to the capital formation process.

In view of the great income gap between the more-developed and less-developed countries, and the very substantial development requirements of the latter, it is hoped that the Development Assistance Committee (DAC) of the OECD will be instrumental in generating a larger total flow of capital funds for development purposes through various national and international programmes as well as private investment. As the more industrialised nations enjoy increasing income levels, their ability to participate in assisting the less-developed world will naturally improve.

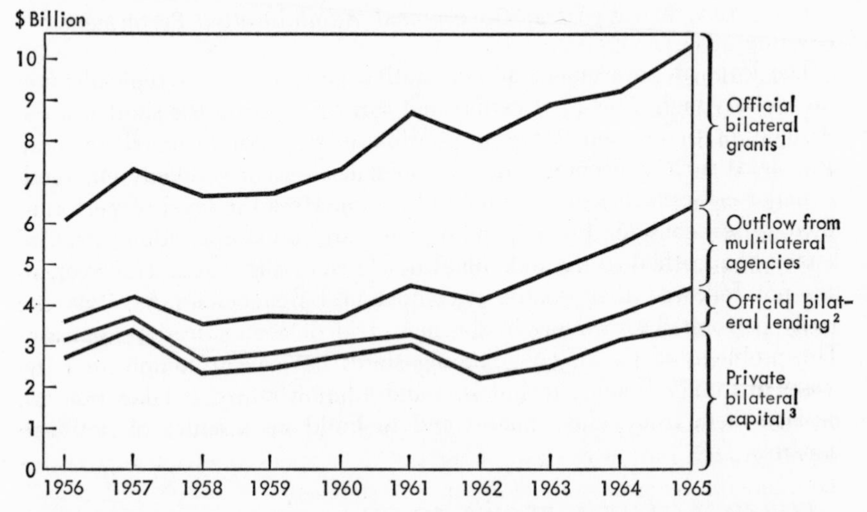

[1] Including grants, reparation and indemnification payments, net loans payable in recipients' currencies, and net transfers of resources through sales against recipients' currencies. [2] Loans with maturities of more than 1 year, net. Also includes other government bilateral long-term capital, net. [3] Including private export credits with maturities of more than 1 year, net.

The Net Flow of Capital from Industrial Countries and International Agencies to Less-Developed Countries

Equally important to making available additional funds for the development of the poorer countries is ensuring that maximum advantage is derived through carefully formulated projects in well-considered sectorial programmes—ideally within the framework of carefully prepared overall development programmes. Qualitative factors may be far more important than the mere size of investment activities in determining the impetus provided to the development process. The less-developed world's landscape is speckled with poorly selected projects with a limited "multiplier" effect. Further, an inhospitable institutional or political environment, an unco-ordinated development plan, ineffectual economic policy or shortages of requisite skills may largely nullify the benefits of costly development projects. To contribute more effective development efforts the DAC has begun to study the efficacy of Members' individual assistance programmes.

PROBLEM OF DEPRESSED EXPORT EARNINGS

Since 1955 exports from the less-developed countries have been expanding at only about half the rate of total world trade. A significant deterioration in the less-developed countries' terms of trade (prices of exports versus prices of imports) took place until 1962, notably since the dissipation in the mid-1950s of the price increases prompted by the Korean War. The price fall has been most severe with respect to those export commodities important to Latin America, Africa and the non-sterling less-developed countries of Asia. However, in 1963 and most of 1964, prices of a number of primary products rose. In spite of a weakening in prices for some primary products in the latter months of 1964, the general level again increased slightly in 1965. In fact, the export earnings of less-developed countries expanded more rapidly in the early 1960s than in the second half of the preceding decade. However, the increase was still smaller than that of the industrialised countries. The lower growth rate of the exports of less-developed countries may be accounted for by growing European self-sufficiency in meat and cereals and a variety of shifts in demand away from the traditional export products of the less-developed nations partly due to the increased incomes enjoyed by the more-industrialised countries as well as the development of synthetic substitute products.

The export trade of the less-developed countries has continued to be dominated by primary commodities. The decreasing share of the exports of the countries in world trade heightens the issue of improving efficiency of production of export products and further underscores the importance of achieving greater economic diversification and particularly of increasing the variety of export products.

It is vital that the more-developed countries increase the export opportunities in their markets for the products of the less-developed nations. This is as important a factor as the flow of capital resources itself. But actions to increase the access of markets to the less-developed nations by various measures, including tariff reductions, have been slow in adoption and have assumed the highest order of urgency.

* * *

TECHNICAL ASSISTANCE NEEDS

The vast technical assistance needs of the less-developed countries have not to date been adequately assessed or programmed by the more-developed nations working in co-operation with the less-developed countries. These technical deficiencies cut across the entire range of required skills and constitute, in a real sense, the limiting factor to a higher rate of real investment. The more effective resolution of this problem deserves urgent attention. There has as yet been no commitment to meet the urgent demand for skills in the less-developed countries commensurate with the magnitude of the problem.

Though happily very recently a somewhat better orientation of studies has manifested itself, the programmes for educating the tens of thousands of students from the less-developed countries who are currently in the schools and universities of the more-developed countries still bear only limited relation to the insistent requirements for skills in their own countries. For example, coming from societies where agriculture constitutes the dominant resource, only some 5 per cent of these students are studying how to advance agricultural technology. There is too little concentration on the mechanical and engineering sciences and undue devotion to the study of the prestige-loaded curricula of law, literature and humanities.

Nothing is more vital than pressing the issue of the *relevance* of educational efforts undertaken on behalf of students of the less-developed nations both overseas as well as in their own countries. The subject matter of the representative school curriculum of the less-developed nations has characteristically been modelled not surprisingly upon that of the more-developed Western nations which reflects a fundamentally different kind of environment and set of needs. Co-ordinated and imaginative action on this front by the OECD countries as well as the United Nations working with the less-developed countries is most important to the issue of development.

INVESTMENT NEEDS

It is commonplace to refer to the great gap between the investment requirements of the less-developed countries and the available flow of resources. Actually, we do not as yet have any satisfactory approximation of this requirement. To calculate it, we should need to make systematic economic development studies of every one of the less-developed nations

—using a uniform methodology, a reasonably consistent set of assumptions concerning domestic and foreign trade, and supply and demand functions for the various sectors of the economy. Feasibility studies would have to be made and evaluated for large numbers of possible agricultural and industrial projects—then sets of priorities established in an integrated pattern of development. The pre-investment infrastructure requirements would have to be planned, programmed and "engineered." Manpower studies would be needed to establish requirements for essential skills.

We know much less than we should about the investment absorptive capacities of the less-developed world. Clearly, as infrastructure is created along with other structural and institutional changes, this absorptive potential will grow. It is vital that the various elements that serve to limit absorptive capacities in the short-run be systematically confronted. This must be undertaken on an individual country-by-country basis. As a corollary to the foregoing effort to expand the investment potential, consumption must be subordinated to the accumulation of capital resources to apply to development purposes. Governments are frequently inclined to shy away from the political hazards of difficult decisions in the field of taxation, fiscal policy, agricultural reform and the gamut of actions required by an ambitious development programme. Vested interests would invariably be obliged to make significant sacrifices, with the clear prospect of more to follow and the assurance of a decline in their traditional influence and authority.

CONTAINING THE POPULATION EXPLOSION

The White House Conference
on International Cooperation

Underlying the issues raised at UNCTAD was the broad series of problems that have been created by the rapid growth of population in the poor countries since the end of World War II. This growth, stemming from a continuation of high birth rates and a sharp post-war decline in mortality, reflecting medical and public health advances, has, in effect, worked against the development goals of thickly settled countries. India, Ceylon, and Pakistan are standard examples. Furthermore, the prospect of continued high rates of population growth promises to create similar problems for many more countries over the next few decades. In this report, a group of prominent Americans have proposed that population control be elevated to a major element in United States relations with developing countries.

THE PROBLEM WE FACE

The facts about the world population explosion are now well known. It took hundreds of thousands of years, from the beginning of life on earth to the beginning of this century, for the population of the world to reach 1.5 billion. In the first two-thirds of this century, this number doubled to the present total of something over 3 billion. In the last one-third of this century, if present trends continue, this figure will more than double to over 7 billion.

. . . The results of population growth are ever more ominous in the

White House Conference on International Cooperation, "Containing the Population Explosion," December, 1965, in *Blueprint for Peace*, ed. Richard N. Gardner (New York: McGraw-Hill Book Company, 1966), pp. 127-40. The Committee that wrote this report included Richard N. Gardner (Chairman), Eugene R. Black, Cass Canfield, Leslie Corsa, Jr., Gardner Cowles, A. W. Dent, William H. Draper, Mrs. Albert D. Lasker, David E. Lilienthal, John D. Rockefeller, 3d, Mrs. Edith S. Sampson, George N. Shuster, and Aaron Stern.

less-developed countries of the world. The average annual increase of population in these countries is approximately 2.5 per cent—sufficient to double population every twenty-eight years. In many countries the annual growth rate has reached 3 per cent or more. In Latin America, the region of the world where population growth is highest, total population will rise from something over 200 million today to approximately 600 million at the end of the century if present trends continue.

Public discussion of the population problem has focused attention on the relation between the number of people and the supply of food. In the less-developed areas as a whole, food production has barely kept pace with population growth—and in Latin America, food production per capita has actually declined. The Food and Agriculture Organization has estimated that world food production will have to increase at least threefold by the end of the century to provide an adequate diet for the world's increased numbers. Such an increase seems impossible without a thoroughgoing transformation in existing agricultural institutions and techniques in the less developed areas.

Thus—as a consequence of present population trends—the threat of starvation in many countries is very real. Yet the reason for reducing present rates of population growth in the less-developed countries is not exclusively—nor even primarily—that of avoiding starvation. These countries, whose citizens have an average income of little more than $100 a year, are seeking rapid increases in their living standards. To achieve these increases they must achieve a substantial rate of investment as well as meet their current consumption needs. Yet all many of these countries can do is enlarge total economic product as fast as the additional mouths to feed—so that little or nothing is left over for additions to capital stock.

* * *

Nor can the menace of population growth be calculated in economic terms alone. For the United States and the world, the measure of progress should not be the growth of aggregate statistics, nor even the growth of per capita living standards, but the degree by which each person is assured the ingredients of a full and satisfactory life. These ingredients include not merely the basic necessities such as food, housing, shelter, health and education, but the satisfaction of political, cultural and spiritual needs that are fundamental to all men.

U.S. Ambassador to the United Nations Arthur J. Goldberg put the matter eloquently in his address to the twentieth UN General Assembly:

The ultimate object of any organized society, domestically or internationally, is man—the individual. The effect upon his lot, his fate, his well-being—that will remain the final measure of our success—and our failure. And if we talk about the competition between states, that is the only worthwhile competition —as to which system, which society, best improves the lot of man and upgrades human dignity.

* * *

From this broader perspective, it is apparent that in many countries population growth—even when accompanied by modest increases in per capita income—may threaten the basis of the good life and perhaps the very foundations of civilized society. The population increase and migration from the countryside have outstripped the capacity of many of the world's great cities to supply minimum levels of housing, sanitation, education and transportation. Uncontrolled fertility has been accompanied by increasing resort to abortion—both legal and illegal. Moreover, increasing numbers of illegitimate children are growing up without the benefits of family life. These conditions multiply individual frustrations and take their toll on society in the form of delinquency, crime, revolution, and even war.

The evidence available from history and the social sciences suggests that man, given the opportunity, will liberate himself from rates of population growth which threaten such serious consequences for the social order. Experience in the United States and abroad indicates that most men and women will limit the number of their offspring if they have an opportunity to do so.

In our judgment, freedom to limit family size to the number of children wanted is a basic human right. Yet this basic right does not yet exist, or cannot yet be implemented, in many parts of the United States and in many other countries of the world. It has been estimated that nearly two out of every three couples in the world today lack access to family planning information and services.

The central aim of U.S. policy in the field of population should be to correct this state of affairs—to make the information and the means for family planning available to all who wish to have them. Fortunately, there are now methods for the regulation of pregnancy that are acceptable and appropriate in every cultural and income level both in our own country and abroad. Each individual should have the opportunity to limit his family size through free choice among all the means that are available.

A free society must necessarily make free choice rather than coercion the basis of its population policy. But time is of the essence. The rate of growth of world population is so great—its consequences are so grave—that this may be the last generation which has the opportunity to cope with the problem on the basis of free choice.

Unfortunately, there are no quick and simple solutions to the many problems associated with rapid population growth. It will take time before appropriate measures for the limitation of births can be made available to all who would make use of them. And even if birth rates decline, future increases in population will result from the population growth of the past as more people pass through the childbearing years. Moreover, the application of modern science and medicine in less developed countries will further reduce the death rate and spur population growth.

Thus the United States must base its policy on the assumption of large and continuous increases in population both at home and abroad. Family planning will not quickly or easily alter the demographic facts of life. Nor can it be a substitute for other measures to preserve and extend human dignity—such as the war on poverty at home and economic assistance to less developed countries abroad.

Nevertheless, the success with which the world applies a policy of voluntary family planning in the next few years can spell the difference between rates of population growth that are compatible with human dignity and those that spell certain misery for an increasing minority in the United States and a growing majority overseas. In the words of Dr. B. R. Sen, Director-General of the Food and Agriculture Organization:

> The next 35 years, till the end of the century, will be . . . a most critical period in man's history. Either we take the fullest measures both to raise productivity and to stabilize population growth, or we will face disaster of an unprecedented magnitude. We must be warned that in the present situation lie the seeds of unlimited progress or unlimited disaster, not only for individual nations but for the whole world.

WHERE WE STAND

There are at least three prerequisites to effective action on the world population problem—(1) adequate *information* about the demographic facts, the economic and social implications of those facts, and the means of influencing the demographic facts through changes in individual attitudes toward childbearing; (2) *techniques* of family planning which are acceptable and effective in different economic, social, cultural and religious environments; and (3) the *implementation* of nation-wide *action programs* of family planning.

Significant progress has been made during recent years in each of these key areas:

In the field of *information,* much has been done in the United States and overseas to improve knowledge in all aspects of the population problem—in census taking and vital statistics, in the ability to project future population trends, in the inter-relationship between population trends and economic and social development, in individual attitudes toward childbearing, and in the factors which may cause these attitudes to change. . . . [E]xtensive private effort has been supplemented by growing support from governments and international organizations. The Agency for International Development, in collaboration with the U.S. Public Health Service, the Bureau of the Census, and universities, has supported research, training institutes, and conferences on population problems. The governments of other countries, in many cases with encouragement and support from AID, have greatly improved their capacities in such fields as census taking, the gathering of vital statistics, the projection of changes in population size and composition, and the analysis of the consequences of such changes for their overall economic plans as well as for particular sectors such as health and education.

National and bilateral efforts are now strongly supplemented by the work of the United Nations and its family of agencies. . . .

Progress has also been impressive in the development of family planning *techniques.* Research in recent years has sought to improve the reliability of the rhythm method for the regulation of pregnancies. Laboratory studies and extensive field trials, including some in the developing countries, have confirmed the effectiveness of birth control pills (progestational steroids) and plastic intra-uterine devices (I.U.C.D.). The I.U.C.D. in particular has stimulated hope for relatively rapid reductions in birth rates in less developed areas because it is cheap, highly effective, and requires only a single act—insertion of the device—to bring long-lasting protection from pregnancy.

Research by government and by many of the private organizations mentioned above, especially the Population Council and the Ford and Rockefeller Foundations, has helped significantly in the development of these and other effective techniques for the regulation of pregnancy. The World Health Organization has also begun a program of research in human reproduction which should help to broaden the narrow geographic base which now exists for work in this field.

Progress has also been made, though much more slowly, in the actual *implementation* of family planning programs.

. . . An increasing number of less developed countries have instituted nation-wide programs of family planning. Korea, the Republic of China, and Tunisia are well on the way to establishing effective family planning programs. The United Arab Republic, India, and Pakistan are significantly expanding their efforts—although these still reach only a small fraction of the population. Turkey is about to embark on a national effort after repeal of a forty-year-old law against contraception. Pilot projects are under way in Malaysia and Ceylon.

Until very recently, no government in Latin America, with the exception of Chile, had an active program of family planning. Now this situation is beginning to change. Increasing emphasis has been placed on the population problem in meetings of the Alliance for Progress, and the first Pan-American Assembly on Population Problems was held in Colombia in August, 1965. Peru and Venezuela have now established population units within their Ministries of Health, and Colombia has done the same within its Association of Medical Faculties.

President Kennedy committed the United States to the task of making more knowledge about family planning more available to the world. With his encouragement, the United States initiated a policy of providing assistance in the population field to other countries upon request. In his State of the Union Message of January 4, 1965, President Johnson pledged to "seek new ways to use our knowledge to help deal with the explosion in world population and the growing scarcity of world resources." Under his leadership, the Executive Branch is now fully committed to action on the population problem.

. . . The United States is not the only Government prepared to offer assistance in support of family planning programs overseas. Sweden has been doing so for years, and Great Britain and Japan have recently entered the same field. The Development Assistance Committee (DAC) of the Organization of Economic Cooperation and Development (OECD) has begun to study the implications of population growth for the assistance programs carried on by its member countries. This may well stimulate the expansion of existing assistance programs in the population field and the establishment of new ones.

* * *

These achievements—in the study of population problems, in the development of family planning techniques, and in the actual establishment of family planning programs—are all impressive. But they are not enough. More needs to be done in each of these areas if the world is to cope effectively with the population problem. Having examined what has already been done, we now need to consider the tasks that lie ahead.

FUTURE GOALS—AND HOW TO ACHIEVE THEM

The overriding objective toward which population policy should be directed can be stated simply—it is to defend and enlarge the essential values of modern civilization now threatened by unrestricted population growth, by putting every couple in a position to determine the family size it wants.

It would be contrary to everything our country stands for to implement a population policy by coercion. U.S. policy in this area should be guided by two fundamental principles: dissemination of knowledge and freedom of choice. The fact that at present substantial groups in the United States and overseas do not have access to family planning information and services by virtue of limited educational, economic, or other circumstances, constitutes a particularly objectionable form of *de facto* discrimination. Government action to eliminate such discrimination enlarges human freedom, promotes individual dignity, and more effectively implements the historic purposes of our country.

To accomplish these objectives, the three elements of population policy must be implemented with a new sense of urgency:

We must intensify our efforts to increase *information* on all aspects of the population problem. Private organizations should be encouraged to continue their efforts in this field. The U.S. Government should substantially increase its aid to other governments, on their request, in ascertaining the facts about their population situation and the significance of these facts for economic and social development. AID, in cooperation with the Bureau of the Census, should expand its training of foreign personnel in the collection, processing, publication, and analysis of essential data. United Nations agencies should also be encouraged to enlarge their research and technical assistance in this field. International organizations can be particularly valuable in building a broad consensus on population problems and what should be done about them.

Special attention needs to be given also to the problem of communicating family planning information. Family planning programs can only be effective to the extent that they motivate individuals to utilize available techniques for regulating pregnancy. In many areas of the world where birth rates are high, much more needs to be known about how to adapt educational programs to the needs and values of the people.

More attention needs also to be given to the administration and management of effective population programs. Strong research and evaluation units should be established close to the top administrative structure of official agencies to assure that modern techniques of management planning are being fully applied in implementing population programs.

Work should be greatly expanded in the search to improve existing *techniques* of regulating pregnancy. More effort is needed to increase the reliability of the rhythm method, to enhance the effectiveness of the intra-uterine device, and to discover other methods of family planning. The research programs supported by private agencies, by the United States and other governments, and by the World Health Organization in the field of human reproduction should be enlarged as rapidly as possible in order to stimulate further progress in family planning techniques.

The need for intensified effort is greatest of all in the actual *implementation* of family planning programs. The various U.S. agencies concerned with population problems need more staff and funds to meet their growing responsibilities in this critical field. Moreover, the work of these agencies could be made more effective through high-level coordination.

As foreign governments initiate and expand nation-wide programs of family planning, they will increasingly call upon the United States for assistance. The governments of Pakistan, India, and Turkey, for example, have already indicated a desire for U.S. financial support of programs to train family planning workers in large numbers; for U.S. consultants in all fields bearing on the development of country-wide family planning programs; for funds to supplement professional salaries for family planning workers; and for transportation and mass communication equipment.

U.S. direct support of overseas family planning programs in these and other ways should be greatly expanded. We should remember, however, that family planning programs are dependent in the long run on a nation's network of health and social services. An enlargement of U.S. assistance to help other countries strengthen health and social services would not merely be desirable for its own sake; it would provide the essential foundation for the implementation of population policies.

THE WORLD FOOD PROBLEM

President's Science Advisory Committee

The problem of the population explosion discussed in the previous selection is matched by another concern: the ability of the world to produce enough food to maintain the vastly increased world population that now seems in prospect by the end of this century.

In this 1967 report to President Johnson, a distinguished group of agricultural experts states the nature of the problem and possible lines of solution. The report emphasizes that there is no panacea for the world food problem, and that the dangers of mass malnutrition and even starvation are so great that "a massive, long-range, innovative effort, unprecedented in human history will be required to master it."

THE GENERAL PROBLEM

We have been unable to devise any new or original statement of the world food problem. The subject has been treated so thoroughly in orations and editorials during the past two decades that both its size and significance tend to be obscured by rhetorical overkill. All has been said before and said extremely well; all has been repeated, reiterated, and rephrased. The stark misery of hunger, the ravages of malnutrition, the threats of civil strife, social unrest, and political upheaval posed by food shortages, and the shadow cast by impending famine have all been portrayed in urgent and compelling terms. The need for the United States, other developed nations, international agencies, and voluntary institutions to help the hungry nations has been pointed out time after

President's Science Advisory Committee, "The World Food Problem," Vol. I, *Report of The Panel on World Food Supply* (Washington, D.C.: The White House, May, 1967), 3-15. The members of this group of agricultural experts were: Ivan L. Bennett, Jr. (Chairman), H. F. Robinson, Nyle C. Brady, Melvin Calvin, Milton S. Eisenhower, Samuel A. Goldblith, Grace A. Goldsmith, Lowell S. Hardin, J. George Harrar, James G. Horsfall, A. T. Mosher, L. Dale Newsom, William R. Pritchard, Roger Revelle, Thomas M. Ware, and Stuart G. Younkin.

time. Insofar as the citizens of the developed countries of the West are concerned, this obligation to aid the less fortunate of the earth has been accepted without argument and they seem to assume that they are already supporting effective programs which will finally alleviate the problem. So repetitively has the problem been brought to the attention of the American public during the past several years that they seem almost to have lost the ability to respond to the stimulus; they are aware of the existence of the problem, they converse about it from time to time, but there is no longer any depth of understanding or concern. The situation has been aptly put:

> A nation conditioned by affluence might possibly be suffering from compassion fatigue, or from conscience sickness, the peril of narrowing our field of vision to leave out the unpleasant view of life disfigured by hunger.[1]

* * *

Throughout our deliberations and our efforts to respond to the President's directive, we have continually asked ourselves, "Why is the race between food and population being lost?"

Several factors have contributed:

1. The overall problem of the world food supply is so large and so extremely complex that it is almost impossible for the casual or even the moderately concerned observer to comprehend its true dimensions or to grasp its intricate interrelationships with the many other aspects of economic growth and development.

2. Despite its true complexity, the problem, at first glance, seems deceptively straightforward and is, therefore, unusually susceptible to oversimplification. Because eating and even farming seem readily understandable to the average citizen in a developed country such as the United States, the temptation to act on the basis of superficial or incomplete information is almost irresistible. This leads to seizure and overemphasis upon panaceas and piecemeal "solutions" which are inapplicable, ineffectual, or inadequate. The cumulative delays engendered by false starts and stop-gap measures mask the requirement for broad and effective programs, tailored to the demands and dimensions of the overall problem.

3. The details of the task involved in increasing food production to meet world needs have never been charted with the clarity and exactness that the available information will permit. The problem has been treated dramatically but incompletely—usually to incite short-term

[1] Norman Cousins, *Saturday Review*, March 25, 1961.

action for humanitarian reasons. A wholehearted response to an *incomplete proposal,* however, lulls the participants into an unjustified feeling of security that the problem is coming under control.

4. Food shortage and rapid population growth are separate, but interrelated problems. The solutions, likewise, are separate, but related. The choice is not to solve one or the other; to solve both is an absolute necessity. The current tendency to think of food production and fertility control as alternative solutions to a common problem is dangerously misleading.

5. The twin problems of food and population imbalance have one feature in common that adds immeasurably to the difficulties of achieving control. Their eventual solution is crucially dependent upon success in convincing millions of citizens in the developing nations to take *individual* action. Fertility control cannot be achieved by declarations of government policy or by executive decree although adoption of a policy and the provision of information, instruction, and materials are obviously needed and are helpful. Similarly, political declarations concerning agricultural productivity are ineffective unless individual farmers can be convinced to adopt the necessary improved practices. The provision of these personal incentives is a task that encompasses a vast array of social, economic, and political considerations which differ between countries and within countries. Indeed, the very fabric of traditional societies must be rewoven if the situation is to change permanently.

6. The eventual alleviation of world hunger will require many years. It is dependent on far-reaching social reforms and long-range programs of hard work which offer no promises of quick and dramatic results of the type so helpful in maintaining enthusiasm for a concerted, difficult undertaking. The results cannot be seen as a dedication of new buildings, as a successful launching into space, or as other spectacular, "newsworthy" events to punctuate the year in and year out toil.

7. The problem of food production is but one part, albeit a very important part of the enormous problem of economic development in the poor nations. As the years have passed, the great expectations which ushered in our foreign assistance programs, fresh on the heels of the heady successes of the Marshall Plan, have not been realized. Domestic political constraints have so eroded the program and the agency responsible for it that there remains virtually no possibility of commitment to long-range, coordinated action, dedicated to the systematic solution of a series of interrelated problems, none of which can be

solved in isolation from its fellows. The original emphasis upon technical assistance has been so diluted that it is almost correct to say that this form of aid, indispensable to the accomplishment of increases in food production, now receives little more than lip service. Despite chronic reiterations of the need to involve private industry in economic assistance, no significant progress in engaging this rich reservoir of resources and skills can be reported at this time.

> The chief handicap faced by all is the impatience of the modern fast moving world . . . expressed in the desire of philanthropists (individual, foundation, national, and international) for concrete evidence of good they are doing; expressed in the hope of the specialist during a tour of 1½ or 2 years, to leave a permanent mark upon the culture that has been evolving for 1½ or 2 millenia.[2]

* * *

In agricultural development as well as in other areas of assistance to a developing country, the political stability and predominant attitudes of the recipient government are of crucial importance. Most American citizens are thoroughly familiar with the constraints and disruptions that domestic political conditions within a developing country can create for aid programs. Recent history is replete with episodes which try our patience and frustrate our good intentions.

In contrast to these more obvious and better publicized difficulties at the political level, the obstacles posed by traditional culture, social structure, religious beliefs, and the long-established habits and customs of many developing countries are rarely considered in truly realistic terms. To understand, much less to accept these constraints is particularly difficult for Americans who remain among the citizens of Western Nations the least cosmopolitan and least tolerant of delay. The problem of ethnological differences has been epitomized:

> In one country, steel plows are introduced where previously a pointed stick had served. The farmers accepted them with polite gratitude and use them as ornaments but not for plowing. Why? These plows require two hands and the farmers are accustomed to using only one, the other being used to guide the bullock. A more productive variety of rice cannot be introduced in part of Nepal, where it is needed and very well suited to climate and soil, because the grains cling a bit more to the stalk and a new threshing technique would be used. But threshing is a family or community undertaking involving social and

[2] H. E. Thomas, "Cultural Control of Water Development; Role of Science and Technology in African Development," N.A.S. Panel Meeting, San Francisco, 1963.

ritual as well as mechanical activities. Running water in peoples' houses is not accepted because the village well is a social center, as well as source of water . . . It would not be difficult to put together a large list of such minor failures nor to include in it some major ones. If these seem improbable or easily overcome, the reader might review the introduction of an innovation, say the fluoridation of water, into our own technologically highly sophisticated society. He might also consider the willingness with which Christians, out of Christian motives, will help to reduce infant mortality and disease in a distant, non-Christian country and how unwilling they may then be to help control the population explosion that inevitably results.[3]

* * *

PRINCIPAL FINDINGS AND CONCLUSIONS

This report defines and directs attention to a threatening problem of the global environment in which the United States and all nations must dwell together—the declining condition of more than two-thirds of the human race.

The Panel's detailed analysis of the world food problem has led to four basic conclusions:

1. The scale, severity, and duration of the world food problem are so great that a massive, long-range, innovative effort unprecedented in human history will be required to master it.

2. The solution of the problem that will exist after about 1985 *demands* that programs of population control be initiated now. For the immediate future, the food supply is critical.

3. Food supply is directly related to agricultural development and, in turn, agricultural development and overall economic development are critically interdependent in the hungry countries.

4. A strategy for attacking the world food problem will, of necessity, encompass the entire foreign economic assistance effort of the United States in concert with other developed countries, voluntary institutions, and international organizations.

THE NATURE OF THE WORLD FOOD PROBLEM

The world's increasingly serious nutritional problem arises from the *uneven distribution* of the food supply among countries, within countries, and among families with different levels of income. Global statistical surveys, based upon total food produced per person, suggest that there

[3] Francis E. Dart, "The Rub of Cultures," *Foreign Affairs,* January 1963, p. 365.

is no world-wide shortage of food in terms of quantity (calories) or quality (protein) at the moment. But in the developing countries, where two-thirds of the world's population live, there is overwhelming clinical evidence of undernutrition (too few calories) and malnutrition (particularly, lack of protein) among the people. Clearly, millions of individuals are *not* receiving the amounts of food suggested by average figures.

Many South Asian and Latin American countries, for example, have average diets which are nutritionally inadequate according to minimum standards of the United Nations Food and Agriculture Organization (FAO). In these regions, surveys show that the poorest 25 per cent of the people consume diets with caloric and protein contents that are only about three-fourths of the country average and fall far below calculated nutritional requirements. It is in these low income groups that overt malnutrition is found, particularly among the most susceptible groups: infants and preschool children, pregnant women, and nursing mothers.

POPULATION GROWTH AND FOOD NEEDS

1. Population and food problems center directly in the already poor, already diet-deficient countries where food production is low and population growth rates are high. In these developing nations, under the best of circumstances, food needs will at least double within the next two decades.

2. The disproportionate additional need for food in the developing countries cannot be solved by successful programs of family planning alone during the next 20 years. This mathematically demonstrable fact of demography *must not* be interpreted to indicate that population control measures are inherently ineffective or in any way secondary in importance to increasing food production. On the contrary, the Panel's estimates simply show that the impact of successful family planning is cumulative and makes itself felt in the size of the next generation.

For example, the difference in our high and low estimates for world population in 1985 is only 385 million (5.03 billion and 4.65 billion). The difference is greater in later decades and is 1.15 billion in the year 2000 (7.15 billion and 6.0 billion).

To avoid a continued worsening of the population-food situation during the years beyond 1985, that may even reach an economically or ecologically irreversible state of imbalance, *it is imperative to institute intensive programs of family planning now.*

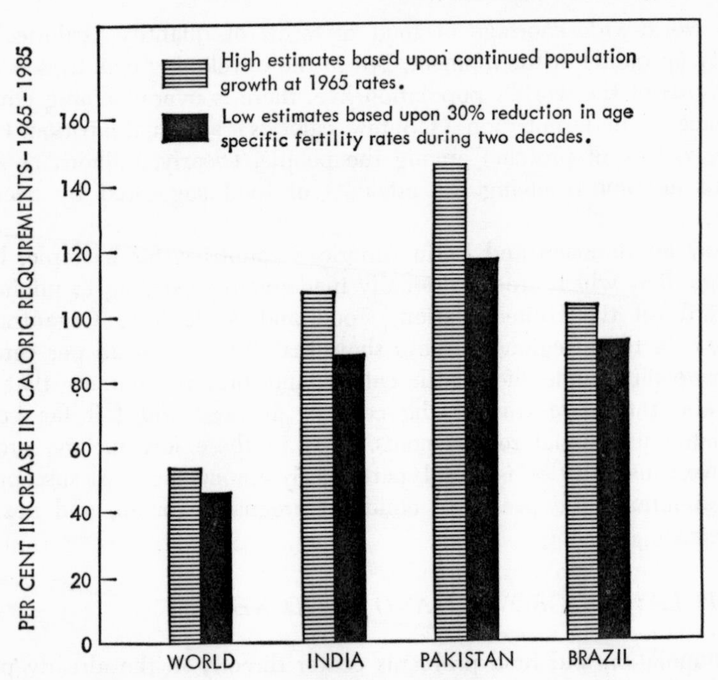

Projection of Caloric Requirements for the World, India, Pakistan, and Brazil [Art Redrawn]

The Panel is unanimous in supporting and urging, in the strongest terms, continuing and increasing emphasis upon research, technical assistance, and capital funding in family planning. Only by such continuing emphasis and effort can the outpacing of food production by population growth be avoided as a problem that might continue well into the next century. The long lag-period that necessarily precedes the main effect of programs of family planning adds to the urgency of the need for action now.

The world food problem is not a future threat. It is here now and it must be solved within the next two decades. If it is solved during this time, it will be manageable for the years thereafter.

This report, then, is addressed to the grim reality of the food shortage that will occur during the next 20 years (actually 1965/66 to 1985/86) before programs of family planning can be expected to bring about long-term amelioration of the problem by reducing world population growth.

* * *

SUBSISTENCE FARMING AND COMMERCIAL AGRICULTURE

In countries where, for centuries, farming has been traditionally at a *subsistence* level, intended to produce food and fiber only for family or local needs, the urgent problem of converting individual farmers to a *commercial* system in which production is primarily for markets at a distance from the farming area has been superimposed upon the other demands of modernization. The cornerstone of economic progress of any nation is the development of its natural resources and manpower. Many of the developing nations must concentrate on agricultural resources as the foundation for building self-sustaining, productive national economies. Conversely, the growth of the entire national economy will be essential in the future to increase agricultural production, which will depend critically on the farmer's ability to purchase fertilizers, tools, high-yielding seeds, pest controls, and irrigation water. To be able to purchase the required materials, farmers will need to sell a major portion of their harvests, which means that there must be increasingly prosperous customers who can buy farm products.

To persuade farmers to accept the techniques and methods of modern agriculture is a formidable and complex undertaking. Farmers in traditional subsistence economies are understandably wary of assuming new risks because they are so close to the margin of survival. If a farmer is to invest in the modern inputs of improved seeds, fertilizers, and pesticides that are essential to increasing the output of his land, these resources must be easily available to him, a system of farm credit must be established so that he can afford to purchase them, he must be instructed in the proper and economic utilization of these materials, he must be reassured that he will be compensated for possible losses incurred in the process of innovation, and, above all, he must be shown that the potential payoff is worth the risk. Land tenure policies should not be such that his landlord will profit and he will not. Government pricing policies should not favor the consumer at the expense of the producer.

All of these factors enter into the vital matter of providing incentives to the farmer to increase production for the market. Fundamentally, it appears that many nations are under-utilizing the power of the market economy. Needed inputs for modern agricultural production are scarce, unreliable in availability, and expensive in relation to the prices of farm products. For example, a bushel of rice will pay for four times as much fertilizer in the United States as it will in Egypt and more than twice as much as it will in Thailand or India.

Both producers *and* consumers are responsive to prices and to income if governments will recognize and use the market mechanism. The Mexican government has recognized this fact in pricing policies and this is a major reason for the growing promise of the Mexican agricultural development program.

To induce farmers to change, the potential payoff must be high—not 5 to 10 per cent but 50 to 100 per cent. Adoption of deep wells for supplemental irrigation in West Pakistan is an example. In five years, nearly 32 thousand private "tube" wells were installed, at a cost of $1,000 to $2,500 each, on farms no larger than 25 acres in the cotton and rice regions of the former Punjab. A private investment of $50 million was made by traditional farmers without government subsidy. Why? The wells typically paid for themselves in two years. If the payoff is large enough, farmers will change.

THE EFFECTS OF URBANIZATION

The enormous increase in nonfarm population in the diet-deficient countries has aggravated the food problem further by making it necessary to develop distribution systems to move more and more food into the cities from the producing areas. This requires the establishment of transportation, storage, processing, and marketing facilities on an unprecedented scale in economies which are already stretched to their limits.

The growth of large cities is a well-recognized characteristic of developed nations but it is not generally realized that the trend toward urbanization is fully as strong in the developing countries. As early as 1950, more than one-third of the world's cities with populations exceeding 100 thousand were in Asia and the exodus from rural areas has accelerated each year since.

The shift of people from farms to cities in the United States and Western Europe has resulted primarily from the reduction in rural labor requirements brought about by advances in modern agricultural technology and increased labor requirements of industry. In the developing countries population growth alone has heightened the frequency with which families leave the overcrowded, poverty-stricken countryside, hoping to find a livelihood in the city. The results in most developing nations have been growing slums and unemployment since unskilled labor is overabundant in both rural and urban areas.

FOOD CUSTOMS AND TABOOS

Dietary habits are established early in life and, in the highly traditional cultures of the developing countries, food selection and diet more often reflect religious and social beliefs than they do the principles of human nutrition. During the past several years, there have been many commercial programs intended to make unfamiliar new food products available to low-income groups in the developing countries. It has become abundantly clear that it is extremely difficult to change fixed food habits. Market research and feasibility studies must give proper attention both to family income and to existing habits and taboos. It has been demonstrated that dietary customs *can* be changed (e.g., people whose dietary staple has been rice have been persuaded to accept wheat as a supplement or substitute) but success in any such undertaking requires time and a carefully prepared program of consumer education. In summary, *any program to remedy malnutrition which involves changing traditional food habits is highly likely to be ineffective in the short-run and even a long-range plan must be carefully programed for the specific local situation.*

MEETING THE NEED FOR MORE FOOD

For the next several years, any major expansion of the world food supply will be dependent on increased production from conventional sources and upon more efficient utilization of available foodstuffs through reduction of waste and spoilage. *The vast majority of the increased production must take place within the developing countries themselves.*

There Is No Panacea

Periodically, the news media draw attention to ongoing research on systems which offer possibilities as new sources of human food. Because there is a strong tendency to portray these as possible "solutions" to the world food problem and because the public is drawn understandably to such panaceas, this publicity undoubtedly lessens concern about the seriousness of the food supply in the developing nations.

The Panel has examined carefully and in detail the several new processes which are under current study.

* * *

In summary, some nonconventional sources of food [such as products of yeast fermentation, protein extracted from leaves, and processed algae] appear to offer great potential for the long-term but in the judgment of the Panel none of these can be expected to lessen the problem of increasing food production from conventional sources during the next two decades.

Furthermore, the magnitude of the world's food problem is so great that nonconventional sources, when and if they become available, may be needed to supplement rather than supplant modernized agriculture. The problem will be with us for so long, however, that every effort must be made now to invent new processes and develop known ones to produce novel foodstuffs. In order to provide a reasonable probability that the long-range potential of unconventional food sources may be realized within two decades, we must accelerate research on these methods now.

Animal Sources

There are good opportunities for improved production of livestock and increased utilization of fishery resources, including fish farming (agriculture), in the developing countries. These deserve emphasis and exploitation because animals are capable of converting to food different types of by-products and forages that cannot be consumed directly by people and for the significant contribution that they can make to improving the quality of protein in diets and earning foreign exchange. A process of producing fish protein concentrate (FPC) appears to hold promise for the future although major problems of scale, technologies for different species, and consumer acceptability must be solved before its usefulness can be evaluated.

Agricultural Production

It is, therefore, evident that the *bulk of the increase in food supply must come from increased production of farm crops.* There are two ways in which agricultural production can be increased: by bringing more land under cultivation or by increasing yields of land under cultivation.

Until the present time, most of the increase in food production in the developing countries has been achieved by extending traditional farming methods over a larger area of cropland. Substantial opportunities remain to bring additional land under cultivation in the less densely populated areas of Latin America and of Africa, but the vast majority of arable land in Asia is already in use. While there are marginal possibilities for using small additional areas, it is clear that as the population continues to grow, the amount of cropland per person in the Asian countries will diminish progressively.

In Asia, a shift to increasing crop production by intensifying agriculture and using modern methods to improve annual yields on land under cultivation will be mandatory. Even in Latin America and Africa, the increasing cost of clearing additional land may well make it more economical in many regions to concentrate on elevating yields rather than expanding cultivated areas.

To increase yields, a major expansion of irrigation facilities will be necessary to make multiple cropping possible independent of wide variations in seasonal rainfall. It also will be necessary to develop and utilize new, high-yielding varieties of plants, to develop and utilize plants with a higher quality of protein, to increase the use of fertilizers and pesticides, and to employ improved farm machinery. Increased capital investments and increased expenditure on the part of farmers will be required to make these tools of modern agricultural technology available. These are the techniques that have been employed so successfully in the developed countries to transform farming into a *business.*

The transition from traditional farming to modern agriculture will be difficult and expensive for the hungry nations but it is absolutely essential if their food needs are to be met. There is no alternative. . . .

THE TASK AHEAD

. . . The Panel is convinced from its study of the world food problem that food shortages and high rates of population growth in the developing countries are not primary problems. Rather, they are manifestations of a more fundamental difficulty, *lagging economic development in the hungry countries.* We find the prospects for the future both sobering and alarming.

As we now view the situation, the United States faces two choices:

1. The first is for the United States to continue to provide technical and capital assistance and private investment to poor countries willing to make the self-help effort to achieve self-sustaining growth. Our foreign assistance program would then continue to be largely an American effort with coordinating relationships with the United Nations organizations and other international institutions. While this course might lead to some improvement over the status quo, it would not suffice to meet the food problem because, for all of its economic resources, the

United States cannot possibly accomplish the immense task of alleviating the world food problem alone. *This course would be unsuccessful in halting or reversing the rapid deterioration of the population-food situation in the developing countries and the world would continue to lose ground.*

2. *The other alternative is for the United States to take the lead in mounting a global effort,* in concert with other developed nations and with international organizations, that will bring to bear the technical skills and capital resources needed to reverse the downward course of the developing countries and to restore the chance of their peoples for a better life.

We are unanimous in the belief that, at this point in history, a new long-term policy direction is indicated urgently—a policy that deals massively, directly, and effectively with this central problem of today's world.

We are unanimous, also, in the belief *that the United States must assume leadership of the free world and all of its international institutions in a coordinated, long-range development strategy for raising the economic level of the poor nations, thereby meeting the threat of hunger, increasing the volume of world trade and economic activity, and contributing to the achievement of the goal of ultimate importance, a lasting peace.*

Why?

In the Panel's view, the concern of this country for the hungry nations is threefold:

1. *Humanitarian*—We should help the less fortunate simply because they need help and we are able to help them. The benefits of altruism are by no means unilateral. The challenge of a difficult task and the moral uplift that comes only from doing for others are needed to temper and balance the leisure and affluence of American life. The real successes of the Peace Corps center in the fundamentally inspired, collective aim that is exemplified in the late Albert Schweitzer's dictum, "It is only giving that stimulates."

2. *Security*—Populations in the developing countries double in 18 to 27 years; 55 to 88 years are required for populations to double in the developed countries. By the year 2000, if present rates of growth continue, there will be more than four times as many people in the developing countries as are in the developed nations. To avoid a threat to the peace of the world as well as to our own national security, we cannot

afford to be too little and too late with our development assistance. The expectations of the poor are demanding fulfillment. It is to be hoped that some measure of their ambitions can be realized by peaceful means.

3. *A Better Tomorrow for Us, Too*—This is a long-range goal, an economic reason for investment. An important way to expand our own economy in the future will be through further specialization and trade. As nations develop they become trading nations and through trade, both parties to a transaction benefit. Trading partners are likely to be peaceful protagonists.

PART II

Foreign Aid: Theory and Practice

FOREIGN ECONOMIC AID: MEANS AND OBJECTIVES

Milton Friedman

Milton Friedman, Professor of Economics at the University of Chicago, is a particularly vocal and effective advocate of free enterprise and free markets as the dominant elements for promoting economic growth and political freedom. In this essay he applies his ideology to attack the political and economic effectiveness of foreign aid.

. . . Two questions must be answered in judging government economic aid. First, is it likely in fact to promote the economic development of the countries to whom aid is granted? Second, do its political effects in those countries promote democracy and freedom?

The second question, though not much discussed, is easy to answer and admits of little dispute. As it has so far been administered, our aid program has consisted predominantly of grants or loans or provision of personnel or material directly to the governments of recipient countries for specified projects regarded as contributing to economic development. It has thereby tended to strengthen the role of the government sector in general economic activity relative to the private sector. Yet democracy and freedom have never been either attained or maintained except in communities in which the bulk of economic activity is organized through private enterprise.

. . . Many proponents of foreign aid recognize that its long-run political effects are adverse to freedom and democracy. To some extent, they plead special extenuating circumstances. For example, the group in power in a particular country may for the time being be in a shaky

Milton Friedman, "Foreign Economic Aid: Means and Objectives," *The Yale Review,* Summer, 1958. Reprinted by permission of *The Yale Review* and Milton Friedman.

political position, yet its overthrow may mean the assumption of power by anti-democratic forces. And economic aid may help such a government over its temporary political crisis. Their main reply, however, is that economic progress is a prerequisite to freedom and democracy in underdeveloped countries, and that economic aid will contribute to this outcome and thereby on balance promote political freedom. This makes the crucial question, even for political effects, the first, namely, the economic effects of economic aid.

The belief that foreign aid effectively promotes economic development rests in turn on three basic propositions: first, that the key to economic development is the availability of capital; second, that underdeveloped countries are too poor to provide the capital for themselves; third, that centralized and comprehensive economic planning and control by government is an essential requisite for economic development.

All three propositions are at best misleading half-truths. Additional capital is certainly essential for development. And of course the more capital the better, *other things being the same*. But the way in which capital is provided will affect other othings. The Pharaohs raised enormous sums of capital to build the Pyramids; this was capital formation on a grand scale; it certainly did not promote economic development in the fundamental sense of contributing to a self-sustaining growth in the standard of life of the Egyptian masses. Modern Egypt has under government auspices built a steel mill; this involves capital formation; but it is a drain on the economic resources of Egypt, not a contribution to economic strength, since the cost of making steel in Egypt is very much greater than the cost of buying it elsewhere; it is simply a modern equivalent of the Pyramids except that maintenance expenses are higher. Such modern monuments are by no means the exception; they are almost certain to be the rule when funds are made available directly or indirectly to governments that are inevitably under pressure to produce the symbols of modern industrialism. There is hardly an underdeveloped country that does not now waste its substance on the symbol of a government-owned or government-subsidized international airline. And there is hardly one that does not want its own steel mill as yet another potent symbol.

Some monuments are inevitable in the course of economic development and may indeed be politically desirable as tangible and dramatic signs of change. If the appetite for monuments were at once so intense as to make them the first claim on a country's resources and yet so limited and satiable that their extent was independent of the resources available, monument-building might be a costly fact of life but would have little relevance to foreign economic aid. Unfortunately, this is hardly the case. The appetite grows by what it feeds on. The availability of resources at little or no cost to the country in question inevitably stimulates monument-building. Thus while foreign aid grants may in the first instance add to the capital available to a country, they also lead to a notable increase in the amount of capital devoted to economically wasteful projects.

Cannot, it will be asked, these problems be solved by our exercising control over the use of the capital we make available to governments? And would they not be avoided even more directly if we adopted the proposal to make funds available directly to private enterprises? Aside from the political problems raised by any attempt at close control of even the funds we give, the answer is no. In the first place, there is a purely technical difficulty. Our grants are only part of the total capital available to a country and of the funds available to the government. It will do no good to control the use of the one part while exercising no control over the other; the effect would simply be to alter the bookkeeping—whatever we regarded as appropriate projects would be treated as financed with our funds, and the monuments would be built with local funds. Effective control would thus require us to control the whole of the capital investment of the country, a result that is hardly feasible on political grounds. But even if it were, the problem would by no means be solved. We would simply be substituting one central planning group for another. This leads to the third proposition: that central planning by government is essential to economic development.

Before turning to this issue, it will be well to consider the assertion that the underdeveloped countries are too poor to save and provide capital for themselves. Here, too, the alleged fact is most dubious. Currently developed countries were once underdeveloped. Whence came their capital? The key problem is not one of possibility but of incentive and of proper use. For generations, India was a "sink" for the precious metals, as the writers on money always put it. There was much saving, but it took the unproductive form of accumulation of specie. In Africa, natives on the very margin of subsistence have, given a market demand for their produce, extended greatly the area under cultivation, an activity involving the formation of capital, though seldom entering into recorded figures on savings. Domestic capital can be supplemented by foreign capital if the conditions are right—which means if property is secure against both private and public seizure. Many low income countries cannot of course attract foreign capital; in most of these, in fact, locally owned capital is invested abroad, and for the same reason—because there is not an environment favorable to private property and free enterprise. And in this respect, too, government-to-government grants are likely to be adverse to economic development. They strengthen the government sector at the expense of the private sector, and reduce the pressure on the government to maintain an environment favorable to private enterprise. We may and do seek to counteract this effect by using our grants to get "concessions" from the government favorable to private enterprise. But this is seldom anything like a complete offset—the change in the objective power of the government sector is likely ultimately to outweigh by far the imposed restraint on how for the time being it uses that power. The final result of our grants is therefore likely to be a reduction in the amount of capital available from other sources both internally and from the outside.

In short, if any generalization is valid, it is that the availability of capital while an important problem is a subsidiary one—if other conditions for economic development are ripe, capital will be readily available; if they are not, capital made available is very likely to be wasted.

Let us turn now to the proposition that economic development requires centralized governmental control and planning, that it requires a coördinated "development program." This proposition, too, contains an element of truth. Government certainly has an important role to play in the process of development. It must provide a stable legal framework; it must provide law and order, security to person and property. Beyond this, it has an important role in promoting certain basic services, such as elementary education, roads, and a monetary system; it can make an important contribution by extension activities which help to spread knowledge of new and improved techniques. And numerous other activities of the same sort come to mind.

But none of these activities calls for a centralized program for economic development or detailed control of investment. And such a centralized program is likely to be a hindrance, not a help. Economic development is a process of changing old ways of doing things, of venturing into the unknown. It requires a maximum of flexibility, of possibility for experimentation. No one can predict in advance what will turn out to be the most effective use of a nation's productive resources. Yet the essence of a centralized program of economic development is that it introduces rigidity and inflexibility. It involves a central decision about what activities to undertake, and the use of central force and authority to enforce conformity with that decision.

It may well be that in many underdeveloped countries, existing or potential government officials are as competent both to judge what lines of activity will be profitable and to run particular plants as existing or potential private businessmen. There is yet a crucial advantage in letting private business do as much as possible. Private individuals risk their own funds and thus have a much stronger incentive to choose wisely and well. They can be more numerous and they have much detailed information about specific situations that cannot possibly be available to governmental officials. Even more important, however wisely the decisions are made, there are bound to be mistakes. Progress requires that these be recognized, that unsuccessful ventures be abandoned. There is at least some chance that unsuccessful private ventures will be allowed to fail. There is almost none that public ones will be unless the failure is as flagrant as the British ground nuts venture. The mistake will simply be concealed by subsidy or tariff protection or prohibition of competition. If anything is clear from widespread experience with governmental economic activity, it is that a governmental venture, once established, is seldom abandoned. And surely it is almost as clear that governmental officials are less experimental, less flexible, less adaptive, than private individuals risking their own funds.

What is required in the underdeveloped countries is the release of the energies of millions of able, active, and vigorous people who have been chained by ignorance, custom, and tradition. Such people exist in every underdeveloped country. If it seems otherwise, it is because we tend to seek them in our own image in "big business" on the Western model rather than in the villages and on the farms and in the shops and bazaars that line the streets of the crowded cities of many a poor country. These people require only a favorable environment to transform the face of their countries. Instead there is real danger that the inherited set of cultural and social restraints will simply be replaced by an equally far-reaching imposed set of political and economic controls, that one strait jacket will be substituted for another. What is required is rather an atmosphere of freedom, of maximum opportunity for individuals to experiment, and of incentive for them to do so in an environment in which there are objective tests of success and failure—in short, a vigorous, free capitalistic market.

Thus central control would be a poor way to promote economic development even if the central authorities chose individual projects as wisely as private individuals and with the same end in view. In fact, as we have already seen, the government is almost sure to promote other ends—the national and personal prestige that can be attained through monument-building—so that the case against centralized control is even stronger.

The issues we have been discussing are strikingly illustrated in a report submitted in December, 1956 by the M.I.T. Center for International Studies to the Special Senate Committee to study the Foreign Aid Program. The report studies the problem of how to judge whether a country should be given additional aid. The answer is that the criterion should be whether the country is making an "additional national effort" toward economic development. Two, and only two, "rules of thumb" are given for deciding whether this is the case: "one index that national effort is being mobilized for development is the launching of measures to capture a good fraction of increases in income for the purpose of further investment"; another "measure of national effort . . . is the degree to which a country's leaders have worked out an overall development program."

Here are two of the basic propositions we started with. And the striking thing is that by these tests, the United States would never have qualified as a country making an "additional national effort" toward economic development! We have never had explicit "measures to capture a good fraction of increases in income for the purpose of further investment." Nor have our "leaders" ever "worked out an overall development program." And what is true of the United States is true of every other free nation that has achieved economic development. The only possible exceptions are the economic programs worked out after the Second World War by Britain and some other European countries, and these were largely abandoned because they were failures.

The only countries that satisfy the tests suggested by the M.I.T. report are the Communist countries—these all have measures "to capture a good fraction of increases in income for the purpose of further investment" and all have an "overall development program." And none of these has in fact achieved economic development in the sense of a self-sustaining rise in the standard of living of the ordinary man. In the satellite countries, the standard of living of the ordinary man has quite clearly fallen. Even in Russia, the ordinary man is by no means clearly better off now than before the Communists took over, and, indeed, may be worse off even in terms solely of material comforts. While education and health services have clearly improved, food, shelter, and clothing have all apparently deteriorated for the masses. The achievements of which Russia justifiably boasts are to be found elsewhere: in its heavy industries, its military output, and its space satellites—achievements that from the point of view of the consumer classify strictly as monument building.

It thus seems clear that a free market without central planning has, at least to date, been not only the most effective route to economic development but the *only* effective route to a rising standard of life for the masses of the people. And it is eminently clear that it has been the only route consistent with political freedom and democracy. Yet the M.I.T. report and most other writings on the subject simply take the opposite for granted, without even noting that in doing so they are going against the whole of the evidence to date, and without offering a shred of evidence of their own. This is modern mythology with a vengeance.

What is involved here is no less than another phase of the ideological war in which we are engaged. A central premise of the Communist ideology is that the state must exercise comprehensive control and direction over the economic activities of its citizens; a central premise of Western liberalism is that free men operating in a free market can promote their own objectives without the necessity for an all-powerful state.

Foreign economic aid implicitly accepts this premise of the Communist ideology; yet it is intended as a weapon against Communism. Many who favor it as applied abroad would be horrified at the idea of applying its principles at home. If they accept it, it is because they do not understand what it implies or because they take the word of the "experts" that it is the "only" way to win friends abroad. They, and the experts, are in the state of the man who discovered that he had been speaking prose all his life. Loyal Americans that they are, they have unthinkingly accepted a basic premise of the Communist ideology without recognizing it for what it is and in the face of the available evidence. This is a measure of the success of Marxist thought, which is most dangerous precisely when its products lose their labels.

Despite the intentions of foreign economic aid, its major effect, insofar as it has any effect at all, will be to speed the Communization of the underdeveloped world. It may, for a time, keep some of these countries nominally on our side. But neutral or even hostile democracies are less of a threat to the preservation of a free world than ostensibly friendly totalitarian countries.

An effective program to promote a free and prosperous world must be based on our own ideology, not on the ideology we are fighting. What policy would be consistent with our ideology?

The aim should be to promote free markets throughout the world and maximum reliance by all countries on free enterprise in an environment favorable to competition and to individual initiative. We cannot do this by telling other governments what to do or by bribing them to go against their own natures any more than we can force men to be free. What we can do is to set an example and to help establish an international climate favorable to economic and political freedom; we can make it easier for other countries to take the path of freedom if they wish to.

The most important area in which we can do this is foreign trade. Here, in particular, our policies belie our professions. We profess to believe in free competition and free markets, yet we have erected barriers to "protect" domestic producers from competition; we profess to believe in minimal government interference with economic activity, yet our government imposes quotas on imports and dumps exports abroad because of a policy of government support of farm prices. True, we have also reduced tariffs and barriers to trade in many areas, and these actions, ably supplemented by the unintended effects of inflation, have reduced our trade restrictions to their lowest level in many decades. Yet those that remain, as well as the fresh restrictions that have been imposed, particularly on agricultural products, have, I believe, done far more harm to our foreign relations than any good we have done even temporarily by our economic aid. The rest of the world regards us as hypocrites, and they are at least partly right.

Entirely aside from the problem of foreign relations, these policies do us direct economic harm. They prevent us from using our resources as effectively as we might both at home and abroad; they hurt us as well as the rest of the world. A free trader like myself would like to see them abolished for this reason alone—in order to enable us to have a higher standard of living. But this is only part of the case for free trade, and, in the present context, the lesser part.

A major factor pushing underdeveloped countries in the direction of central planning and of autarchy is their lack of confidence in a market for their products. Suppose, they argue, we do follow the route of free enterprise and free trade, concentrate on producing those things we can produce most cheaply, and count on getting the goods we want to consume through international trade. Is not success likely simply to produce increases in import barriers by the United States and other countries so that we find ourselves all dressed up with a fine export industry and nowhere to go? And, under present circumstances, can one say with any confidence that they are wrong? Ask the Swiss watchmakers and English bicycle producers.

* * *

Suppose we were to announce to the world that we committed ourselves to abolish all tariffs, quotas, and other restrictions on trade by a specified date—say, in five or ten years—and that thereafter we would maintain complete free trade. Can there be any doubt that the effects on our international position—both immediately through the announcement effects and ultimately through the long-run economic effects—would be vastly more favorable than those achievable by any conceivable program of foreign economic aid even if one assigns to that aid all the virtues claimed by its proponents? We would be playing from our strength. We would be offering an opportunity to free men to make effective use of their freedom rather than contributing chains to enslave men.

It would, of course, be better if such action were taken by many nations. But it would be a serious mistake for us to link our actions to that of others; the result would be to slow the movement toward free trade to the pace desired by the most recalcitrant member. Far better to move unilaterally. We would benefit economically and politically from a unilateral move, and we might have far more effect on other countries through example than over the conference table.

A movement toward free trade would affect adversely many particular individuals and concerns—those who have invested talent and capital in "protected" industries. But our mobility and adaptability are such that a gradual movement—over the course of, say, ten years—would give the affected individuals ample opportunity to adjust to the new circumstances with little if any loss. The new opportunities afforded by the expansion of world trade, and the more efficient use of our resources involved therein, would benefit many more than were harmed. After all, the transition to free trade over ten years would have far less of an impact than the technological changes that occur decade after decade and that we take in our stride.

As of the moment, we have a bear by the tail in our foreign economic policy—and unfortunately, it is not the Russian Bear. We get little if any political kudos for continuing economic aid—the recipient countries have come to take it for granted and even to regard it as their right. Yet for this very reason, the sudden cessation of aid would be regarded as an unfriendly and hostile act and would arouse great hostility toward the United States. Thus even if one accepts the arguments of the preceding sections, there remains the problem how to achieve the transition from our present policy to the alternative.

The simplest and least undesirable way seems to me to be to make a final terminal grant to each recipient country. The grant should be fairly generous, say something like two to three times the annual grants we have been making to the country. It should be completely unrestricted and preferably made in the form of a dollar—or even better a Swiss franc—balance on which the recipient country can draw as it wishes. In this way, our own involvement in central planning by other countries could be terminated at once, and the government of the recipient country would attach the greatest value to the grant.

The cost of such a termination program would be sizeable in the year of termination. But it would be a once-for-all cost rather than the steady and growing drain to which we appear to be on the verge of committing ourselves.

Foreign economic aid needs to be sharply distinguished from direct military aid and defense support even though it may be hard to classify any particular expenditure. Foreign economic aid consists of grants or loans from our government to other governments or to enterprises in other countries for specified projects regarded as contibuting to economic development. It includes both technical assistance and grants or loans of money.

The objectives of foreign economic aid are commendable. The means are, however, inappropriate to the objectives. Foreign economic aid, far from contributing to rapid economic development along democratic lines, is likely to retard improvement in the well-being of the masses, to strengthen the government sector at the expense of the private sector, and to undermine democracy and freedom. The proponents of foreign aid have unwittingly accepted a basic premise of the Communist ideology that foreign aid is intended to combat. They have accepted the view that centralized and comprehensive economic planning and control by government is an essential requisite for economic development. This view is contradicted by our own experience and the experience of every other free country.

An effective program must be based on our own ideology, not on the ideology we are fighting. Such a program would call for eliminating the inconsistency between the free trade and free enterprise policies we preach and the protectionist and interventionist policies we at least partly practice. An effective and dramatic program would be to commit ourselves unilaterally to achieving complete free trade by a specified and not too distant date. This would do much to promote an environment and international climate favorable to the rapid development of the uncommitted world along free and democratic lines. It would be an act of truly enlightened self-interest.

ECONOMIC AID RECONSIDERED

Charles Wolf, Jr.

Charles Wolf, Jr., head of the RAND Corporation's Economics Department, is an authority on the economic development of South Asia, and is the author of several volumes on foreign aid, including Foreign Aid: Theory and Practice in Southeast Asia *(1960), and* United States Policies in the Third World *(1967). In this article, he makes a strong attack on Professor Friedman's views, as expressed in the previous selection.*

. . . Basically, Friedman's criticisms are not ostensibly concerned with the question of objectives at all. He acknowledges at the outset that it is an appropriate objective of United States foreign policy that the less-developed countries "satisfy their aspirations for economic development as fully as possible in a democratic framework." If economic aid can make a contribution toward this end that is sufficient relative to its costs, it presumably would be justified for Friedman, as it would for me. In fact, if the marginal contribution were sufficiently great, the inference would follow that United States resources devoted to economic aid should be expanded—a proposal which has been made by two "task force" reports on the subject to President Kennedy. The burden of Friedman's argument is not that the objective is unsuitable, but rather that economic aid is an ill-suited means for attaining the objective. And his verdict that aid is ill-suited rests on the emphatically negative answers he gives to two questions: (a) is government aid "likely to promote the economic development of the countries to whom it is granted?" and (b) will its "political effects in those countries promote democracy and freedom?"

The second question, he asserts, is "easy to answer and admits of little dispute." Friedman's own answer is based on the following propositions: (1) aid is extended on a government-to-government basis, and hence

Charles Wolf, Jr., "Economic Aid Reconsidered," *The Yale Review*, Summer, 1961. Reprinted by permission of *The Yale Review* and Charles Wolf, Jr.

tends "to strengthen the role of the government sector relative to the private sector"; (2) "democracy and freedom have never been either attained or maintained except in communities in which the bulk of economic activity is organized through private enterprise"; and, therefore, (3) aid reduces prospects of political evolution along democratic lines in underdeveloped countries.

I believe that Friedman's argument is incorrect on two counts. Its factual assertions are inaccurate; and the conclusion drawn wouldn't logically follow even if the factual assertions were assumed to be accurate.

First, on the facts. It is true that aid is extended on a government-to-government basis, but it is not true that economic aid tends to "strengthen the government sector relative to the private sector." Leaving aside for the moment the conceptual ambiguity of the quoted phrase, the facts are more complex, and less conclusive, than Friedman's assertion implies. Often the effect of aid has been to *reduce* the encroachment on the private sector. The point isn't whether government projects *receive* aid, but whether, in the *absence* of aid, the pinch would fall on public or private projects. Probably it would fall on both, but there are two reasons why pressure on the private sector would very likely be greater than on the public sector. The first reason is that the zeal of governments and peoples in many of the less-developed countries for the development of sectors in which private investment has traditionally been negligible would result in a strenuous effort to sustain public investment at the expense of the private sector, in the absence of aid. The *étatisme* which understandably worries Friedman would very likely be greatly increased in a country like India, if foreign economic aid were eliminated or sharply reduced, by drastic efforts to capture private savings for public investment projects. This isn't to say that some efforts to increase private savings may not be warranted and desirable anyhow. There seems to be fairly widespread agreement, for example, among both Indian and American economists who have studied the problem, that additional taxation, even of a mildly regressive sort, would be both feasible and desirable as a way of increasing the resources available for economic development. But, in the absence of aid, measures to capture additional resources for public projects would very likely become so intense and authoritarian that pressure on the private sector would rapidly erode it.

The second reason is that, in the *absence* of aid from the United States, the underdeveloped countries would be very likely to receive increased aid from the Communist bloc. The fact that the Communist bloc would become the only major source of intergovernmental aid would be as important as the increased amount of Soviet aid. One could argue that, *given* substantial and efficient United States aid programs, additional Soviet bloc aid programs need not be feared and might even be welcomed by the United States, as well as by the recipient countries. But, in the absence of United States aid, the Soviet bloc could exploit the additional influence which its monopolistic position would provide. This influence would surely not be directed toward the growth of a vigorous private sector.

There are other ways in which United States aid to government projects helps the private sector. One way is by widening the market for private sector output as a result of the increased public-sector demand. Another is by increasing the supply of inputs which are complementary to private enterprise. Consider, for example, United States aid for projects like community development, or irrigation, or fertilizer distribution, or river valley development. These are, typically, government-to-government projects, but they generally have the effect of providing inputs which raise the productivity of privately-owned agricultural and industrial enterprise. Would their diminution more seriously weaken the private sector or the public sector? On balance, I would say the private sector. At the least, Friedman's general assertion to the contrary is quite untenable.

Next, consider his assertion that democracy depends on the bulk of economic activity being "organized through private enterprise." I can think of no historical example that obviously negates it, although the assertion does leave open how much comprises "the bulk" of economic activity. But granting this assertion, and even if it were true that aid tends to increase the relative size of the government sector, it does not logically follow that the effect of aid will be adverse to democracy and freedom.

It is a tricky business to estimate how much economic activity is "organized through private enterprise," to use Friedman's term. It can, for instance, be measured in terms of how much of the national product is *produced* by private enterprise and how much by government; or by how much of the final produce is *purchased* by private individuals or institutions, and how much by government; or by how much is *expended* by private income earners and how much by government. The second measure will yield a higher figure for the government sector than the first since, in all non-Communist countries, some of what is purchased by government is produced by the private sector. And the expenditure measure will show the highest share for the government sector, because part of government expenditures represents income transfers (like veterans' bonuses, unemployment benefits, interest on the public debt, etc.) which are not included in government purchases of goods and services.

If one is concerned loosely with the question of the extent of government "influence" or "intervention" in the economy, as Friedman is, the third measure is probably the best of the three simply because it is the largest. Considering the underdeveloped country with the best statistics, India, which is also one with a relatively active government sector, the proportion of central government expenditures in gross national product in 1958 and 1959 was 12.6 per cent and 12.9 per cent, respectively. In the United States by comparison, the corresponding share of federal government expenditures in the national product was 18.8 per cent and 19.7 per cent, respectively. If we add to federal government outlays those by state governments, the resulting share for the United States was 25.1 per cent and 25.7 per cent for 1958 and 1959. In India, the share of gross national product represented by central and state government expenditures was 18.1 per cent and 18.5 per cent for the two years. If the extent of government activity were instead to be measured by product or by purchases rather than expenditures, the figures would be smaller still. However one looks at it, the overwhelming "bulk" of economic activity in India, and to an even greater extent in most other underdeveloped countries, is "organized through private enterprise." The figures above could be doubled and the statement would still be valid.

The point is simply this: even if the effect of economic aid were to increase the relative size of the government sector in underdeveloped countries substantially (a premise which, as we have seen, is highly doubtful), it would still be true, over a wide range of such an increase, that the "bulk of economic activity" would remain "organized through private enterprise." For Friedman's reasoning to hold, we would have to accept the hypothesis that any *increase* in the relative share of the government sector somehow reduces the degree of freedom, or raises the probability that the government sector will eventually encompass the "bulk of economic activity," *even if the increase still leaves the government sector small relative to the economy as a whole.* This is a much stronger hypothesis than the one he explicitly advances. It is one thing to say that democracy requires the *bulk* of economic activity to be in private hands, and quite something else to say that democracy also requires that there be no *decrease* in the share of economic activity in private hands, or that any such decrease reduces the degree of, or prospects for, democracy. As far as I know, there is absolutely no empirical justification for the stronger hypothesis, and Friedman offers none. Some examples seem quite inconsistent with it. In West Germany and Italy, for instance, the private sector was relatively *smaller* in 1959 than it was in the early 1950's, and yet I doubt that Friedman would argue that democracy and freedom have been correspondingly weakened. International comparisons make the stronger hypothesis look still more absurd. The United Kingdom, with a relatively large government sector, would emerge as "less democratic" than West Germany or Italy or India; and the United States as less democratic than West Germany!

The common sense of the matter would appear to be that, in most underdeveloped countries, there is plenty of room for growth in the absolute and relative size of the government sector without compromising prospects for democracy and freedom. Moreover, if expansion in the government sector is itself a response to widespread popular aspirations for accelerated economic growth, the consequence is very likely to be a strengthening, rather than a weakening, of prospects for democratic political evolution in the underdeveloped countries.

To summarize what has been said: A good case can be made for the contention that, as a result of economic aid, the private sector in most underdeveloped countries is very likely to be absolutely and relatively larger than it otherwise would be. Moreover, even if the government sector were to grow relative to the private sector as a *consequence* of aid, rather than independently of aid, within fairly wide limits such growth would be quite consistent with a maintenance of the bulk of economic activity in private hands, simply because the government sector in underdeveloped countries is so small to start with. Finally, whether some growth in the government sector relative to the private sector strengthens or weakens prospects for democracy, is apt to depend on what political, economic, and social changes are accomplished by that growth, and on how responsive the government is to the will of the people—neither of which can be inferred simply from the growth of the government sector alone. Proponents of foreign economic aid shouldn't claim more than this.

Whether or not economic aid results in an expansion in the relative size of the government sector, it remains legitimate to ask, as Friedman does, if such aid is "likely to promote the economic development of the countries to whom it is granted." Friedman again answers, "Emphatically, no," for three reasons: first, the developmental effect of adding to a recipient country's resources is more than offset by the stimulus provided by aid to wasteful use of both the aid and the country's own non-aid resources; second, if a developing country wanted to develop badly enough, it could extract sufficient savings from its own economy to meet its capital requirements without aid; and third, aid tends to sustain or strengthen government planning of economic development, and government planning is the surest way to stifle development. To save space, I have paraphrased his arguments, without, I hope, distorting them. But no matter how they are put, they should be recognized as statements of ideology and doctrine, not of factual or logical analysis.

Consider the first point. Friedman contends that economic aid conduces to wasteful "monument-building" because it makes resources available to underdeveloped countries "at little or no cost." But clearly there are appreciable "costs" attached to aid. I am not thinking here simply of the "hardness" or "softness" of interest and repayment terms, which in most cases I would argue are quite properly lenient, and perhaps should be more so. As long as one accepts the obviously valid assumption that the quantity of aid available isn't unlimited, *there are always appreciable costs attached to aid.* Freshman economics tells us that the "real" cost of using any limited resource for a particular purpose is the returns that are foregone by not employing that resource in its best alternative use. From the standpoint of any recipient country, these "alternative" or "opportunity" costs are positive and large, even if the aid is an outright gift.

Moreover, recognition of the reality of "opportunity costs" doesn't require that the populations or governments of underdeveloped countries attain a high degree of economic literacy. All it requires is that one government ministry be able to recognize that the use of scarce aid resources to build a "monument" desired by another ministry means that much less available for investing in the productive projects desired by the first ministry. And it requires, further, that people outside the government be able to recognize that wasteful use of government resources —whether derived from foreign or domestic sources—means that much less available for meeting the compelling needs of the public itself. Neither of these minimal requirements is unrealistic. Typically, both are actively operative, and their joint effect is generally to conduce toward economic use of the aid that is provided to underdeveloped countries.

There is still another incentive toward efficient use. The relationship between aid-source and aid-recipient is a continuing one. To the extent that the recipient's anticipation of future aid depends on his efficient use of current resources, he will have a strong incentive to limit monuments and waste. As in the case of opportunity costs, the "future-flow" incentive can operate regardless of whether or what repayment terms are incorporated in government-to-government agreements.

In practice, of course, there are many slips and inefficiencies. Anyone familiar with United States or other international aid programs can't ignore them, and shouldn't defend them. But to say, as Friedman does, that aid is typically wasted because it is costless, is not only bad economics, from a theoretical point of view; it is also a wrong-headed characterization of the actual record of government aid programs.

His second point is based on the contention that external aid is really superfluous. The underdeveloped countries are not too poor to provide capital for their own development. After all, "currently developed countries were once underdeveloped," and they managed to eke out a surplus above subsistence requirements in order to provide capital for their development. The currently underdeveloped countries could do likewise, simply by offering sufficient incentives to domestic saving and to foreign investment. Their failure to do so results from a lack of will, rather than an absolute lack of resources. If they had the will, foreign aid would be superfluous. Moreover, Friedman contends, aid is even worse than superfluous, because it tends to "reduce the pressure on government to maintain an environment favorable to private enterprise." Consequently, he concludes, "the final result of our grants is therefore likely to be a reduction in the amount of capital available from other sources both internally and from the outside."

There is an eighteenth-century nostalgia to these arguments, but they deserve reply, both because of their source and because of the extent to which they diverge from currently accepted views. Consider, first, the analogy between currently underdeveloped countries, and the currently developed countries before they developed. From an economic viewpoint, probably the main imperfection in the analogy is that the relationship of income and natural resources on the one hand, to population on the other, is tighter in the currently underdeveloped countries. The physical hardship accompanying self-financing of development in the currently less-developed countries would thus be more acute than it was in the seventeenth and eighteenth centuries in Western Europe, or the nineteenth century in the United States. To some extent, this may be offset by the fact that the currently underdeveloped countries are "late-comers" and hence can draw on technological possibilities that were not available to the early arrivals. But the offset is probably only partial. The economic problems of the currently underdeveloped countries are just harder.

None of this touches the core of what is wrong with Friedman's analogy. The big differences aren't economic, but psychological and political. The currently underdeveloped countries live in a world populated by countries which have already developed, and which display the fruits of their development in higher living standards and greater power. The effect of this demonstration is to heighten the aspirations of the currently underdeveloped countries, and to intensify their impatience for development. The acceptable time period for development is consequently much shorter than in the classical examples of development. Diffusion of suffrage in the underdeveloped countries means that governments which tolerate the pace or the inequalities of seventeenth- and eighteenth-century European development will probably not survive. The crucial political difference characterizing the present development context is the obvious one that the currently underdeveloped countries live in a world in which Communism is a tangibly real alternative route to economic development. Hence, the risk of delayed development is just much greater in the currently underdeveloped countries. In effect, Friedman's analogy is misleading because the urgency of development is greater and the available resources smaller in the currently underdeveloped countries than in the classical examples he has in mind.

But what of the argument that the net effect of foreign aid is to reduce the capital that is available by reducing "the pressure on [recipient] governments to maintain an environment favorable to private enterprise"? Implicit in this assertion is the view that in the *absence* of aid, the "environment" would be more favorable to private enterprise. This prognosis seems to me quite unsupported, and, for reasons I've already mentioned above, unsupportable. In general, the effect of foreign aid, as I have seen it operate in South and Southeast Asia, has been to make foreign exchange more readily available to private enterprise, to lower the cost and increase the supply of publicly-provided inputs to private enterprise, and probably to lower the taxes that otherwise would be levied on individual and corporate incomes. In this connection, it is notable that during the past ten years of India's foreign-aided development plans, private enterprise has been more buoyant and expansionist than ever before. I am not denying that private domestic and foreign enterprises have their troubles in underdeveloped countries, or that governmental bureaucracy accounts for much of these troubles through capricious allocations of foreign exchange and through discriminatory collection of taxes from honest firms. What I am suggesting is that, in the absence of aid, these troubles would probably be more acute. Pressures on private enterprise would intensify, not abate. It is, of course, almost as hard to substantiate this prognosis as Friedman's. But besides the Indian example, I would also note that in every underdeveloped country I am familiar with, private business organizations strongly support the need for and desirability of foreign aid. If their interests were adversely affected by aid, it is quite unlikely that they would do so.

Friedman's third reason for asserting that aid does not in fact promote development is that aid sustains and propitiates centralized government planning, and planning is inherently counterdevelopmental. Planning is counterdevelopmental because it tends to be rigid and inflexible while effective development requires experimentation and flexibility. These characteristics are more likely to be obtained under a system of private enterprise than under government planning, because private enterprise provides strong incentives toward careful choice and toward rapid correction of mistakes.

There is an element of truth in Friedman's argument. But the argument is overstated and incomplete. There are powerful reasons why the case for planning is much stronger than Friedman allows. Some of these reasons concern what economic jargon refers to as "external economies" and "decreasing costs." "External economies" relate to the social benefits produced by a particular activity which are not recoverable or appropriable by the project's owners or investors. The usual examples include education and training, public utilities like roads and river valley development, and public health. Since these benefits are "non-appropriable," they will obviously not enter into private investors' calculations of the profitability of alternative investment opportunities. The consequence will be underinvestment in external-economy-generating activities, and a need for compensating government investment to offset the deficiency. "Decreasing costs" relate to activities which result in lower costs as the scale of the activity increases. Often the scale required for realizing "decreasing costs" entails investment outlays far beyond what is accessible to private enterprise in the underdeveloped countries. And even if the investment requirements were met, "decreasing costs" would preclude the continued existence of many firms and competitive markets. Without going into the technical ramifications of either "external economies" or "decreasing costs," the revelant point is that both considerations will result in underinvestment in potentially high-priority activities under a regime of private enterprise. Government initiative to compensate for these deficiencies will be necessary if available resources, domestic as well as foreign, are to have maximum effect on economic growth.

These reasons for active government planning in the underdeveloped countries are supplemented by other strongly practical considerations. Imperfections and rigidities in the market mechanism are many and notorious in underdeveloped countries. Although improvements in the flow of information and the mobility of capital and labor are possible and desirable in the underdeveloped countries, these rigidities are deep-seated and durable. The real alternative to some government intervention in these countries is not a smoothly functioning free market, but a market pervaded by barriers and rigidities. The distortion in Friedman's argument arises from comparing an ideal model of a free market regimen with casual observation of the worst features of government planning. In the real world of the underdeveloped economies, private enterprise and the free market are neither as flexible or adaptive as Friedman suggests, nor is government planning as rigid and inefficient. Both the market and planning have their justifications and shortcomings. As Edward Mason has put it: "The really good arguments for planning lie in the obvious inadequacies of the market, and the really good arguments for the market rest on the deficiencies of planning."

My conclusions from these remarks are in direct contradiction to Friedman's answer to the question of whether aid is likely to promote economic development. There have been examples of "monument building," but, in general, aid has been productively used, and the institutional mechanisms for extending aid have tended to increase the productive use of non-aid resources as well. It is, moreover, definitely not true that aid leads to wasteful use because it is "costless." The existence of alternative uses for aid means that there are always appreciable costs attached to its use in any wasteful activity. Although the bulk of capital requirements for development must be internally generated, the effect of complete self-financing would very likely be to induce the internal authoritarianism which Friedman wishes to avoid, and encourage the erosion of private enterprise which he wishes to protect. Finally, there are both strong theoretical and practical reasons for expecting and encouraging some degree of government planning in underdeveloped countries. True, planning by government can be rigid and inflexible, as can planning by private enterprise. But, more important, government planning that is rigid and inflexible can be improved. Economic aid is probably a much more appropriate tool for improving the quality of planning than it is for affecting the quantity.

In his zeal to discredit foreign aid, Friedman criticizes two criteria that have often been mentioned by advocates of aid as tests of the eligibility of a recipient country for additional aid. The eligibility criteria he criticizes are, first, whether a recipient is taking "measures to capture a good fraction of increases in income for the purpose of further investment," and, second, the extent to which the recipient has "worked out an overall development program." His criticism takes the form of noting that the United States itself would not have been able to qualify for aid under these criteria during the period of its own initial development, that "the only countries that satisfy [these] tests . . . are the Communist countries," and that none of the Communist countries has in fact achieved a continuing "rise in the standard of living of the ordinary man."

Actually, I agree that the particular aid criteria he refers to are vulnerable to criticism. In fact, I have criticized them elsewhere at length for, among other reasons, giving absolutely no attention to the relative productivity or efficiency of resource use in recipient countries in determining aid allocations among them. But the particular criticisms advanced by Friedman seem to me either misleading or just factually wrong.

The assertion that the United States would not have qualified for assistance under these criteria is true, but pointless. The United States didn't receive intergovernmental aid, and the objectives which motivate aid to the currently underdeveloped countries were quite irrelevant to our development in the nineteenth century. True, Communist countries would qualify under these criteria (though of course they would be disqualified under the implicit additional criterion that the objective of aid is to increase the chances of survival and success of non-Communist political systems). But it is palpably *untrue* that "the *only* countries that would satisfy the tests are the Communist countries." Currently, India, Pakistan, Burma, among others, eminently satisfy the criteria; historically, Japan would have done so.

Moreover, we should be wary about falling into the trap of assuming that anything the Communist countries do or have done is necessarily something we should avoid, or encourage others to avoid. Even if the assumption is often warranted, it sometimes is not. If, for example, the Communists retain a consequential capability to wage war with conventional weapons, it doesn't follow that we should avoid doing likewise or encouraging non-Communist countries to do likewise. If the Communists have tried to plan their economic development and have adopted various measures to capture increases in income for further investment, it doesn't follow that we should discourage the underdeveloped countries from doing so.

Friedman's last point, that none of the Communist countries has achieved increased living standards, is just wrong. Discussions of foreign aid, or of the uses and misuses of development planning in underdeveloped countries, are not advanced by erroneously asserting, as he does, that planned development in Communist Russia has not raised living standards for the mass of the people.

PART III

International Trade and Investment: Theory and Practice

DEVELOPMENT AND UNDERDEVELOPMENT

Gunnar Myrdal

Gunnar Myrdal, the distinguished Swedish economist, author of many landmark works, including An American Dilemma, *has long argued that the effects of the present system of world trade are harmful to the interests of underdeveloped countries. In this excerpt from a series of lectures delivered in Cairo for the National Bank of Egypt, he sets forth the reasons for his views.*

1.—*THE POVERTY OF THE UNDERDEVELOPED COUNTRIES*

. . . Contrary to what the equilibrium theory of international trade would seem to suggest, the play of the market forces does not work towards equality in the remunerations to factors of production and, consequently, in incomes. If left to take its own course, economic development is a process of circular and cumulative causation which tends to award its favours to those who are already well endowed and even to thwart the efforts of those who happen to live in regions that are lagging behind. The Backsetting Effects of economic expansion in other regions dominate the more powerfully, the poorer a country is.

Within the national boundaries of the richer countries an integration process has taken place: on a higher level of economic development expansionary momentum tends to spread more effectively to other localities and regions than those where starts happen to have been made and successfully sustained; and inequality has there also been mitigated

Gunnar Myrdal, "Development and Underdevelopment," *National Bank of Egypt Fiftieth Anniversary Commemoration Lectures* (Cairo: National Bank of Egypt, 1956). Reprinted by permission of the National Bank of Egypt and Gunnar Myrdal.

through interferences in the play of the market forces by organised society. In a few highly advanced countries—comprising only about one-sixth of the population in the non-Soviet world—this national integration process is now being carried forward towards a very high level of equality of opportunity to all, wherever, and in whatever circumstances they happen to be born. These countries are approaching a national harmony of interest which, because of the role played by state policies, has to be characterized as a "created harmony"; and this has increasingly sustained also their further economic development.

Outside this small group of highly developed and progressive countries, all other countries are in various degrees poorer and mostly also less progressive economically. In a rather close correlation to their poverty they are ridden by internal economic inequalities, which also tend to weaken the effectiveness of their democratic systems of government in the cases where they are not under one form or another of oligarchic or forthright dictatorial rule.

The relations between relative lack of national economic integration and relative economic backwardness run, according to my hypothesis of circular cumulative causation, both ways. With a low level of economic development follow low levels of social mobility, communications, popular education and national sharing in beliefs and valuations, which imply greater impediments to the Spread Effects of expansionary momentum; at the same time the poorer states have for much the same reasons and because of the very fact of existing internal inequalities often been less democratic and, in any case, they have, because they are poorer, been up against narrower financial and, at bottom, psychological limitations on policies seeking to equalise opportunities. Inequality of opportunities has, on the other hand, contributed to preserving a low "quality" of their factors of production and a low "effectiveness" in their production efforts, to use the classical terms, and this has hampered their economic development.

On the international as on the national level trade does not by itself necessarily work for equality. A widening of markets strengthens often on the first hand the progressive countries whose manufacturing industries have the lead and are already fortified in surroundings of external economies, while the underdeveloped countries are in continuous danger of seeing even what they have of industry and, in particular, their small scale industry and handicrafts outcompeted by cheap imports from the industrial countries, if they do not protect them.

It is easy to observe how in most underdeveloped countries the trading contacts with the outside world have actually impoverished them culturally. Skills in many crafts inherited from centuries back have been lost. A city like Baghdad, with whose name such glorious associations are connected, today does not harbour any of the old crafts, except some silver smithies, and they have adapted patterns from abroad requiring less craftsmanship; similarly it is only with the greatest difficulties that one can buy a book of Arabic literature, while cheap magazines in English or Arabic are in abundance.

If international trade did not stimulate manufacturing industry in the underdeveloped countries but instead robbed them of what they had of old-established crafts, it did promote the production of primary products, and such production, employing mostly unskilled labour, came to constitute the basis for the bulk of their exports. In these lines, however, they often meet inelastic demands in the export market, often also a demand trend which is not rising very rapidly, and excessive price fluctuations. When, furthermore, population is rapidly rising while the larger part of it lives at, or near, the subsistence level—which means that there is no scarcity of common labour—any technological improvement in their export production tends to confer the advantages from the cheapening of production to the importing countries. Because of inelastic demands the result will often not even be a very great enlargement of the markets and of production and employment. In any case the wages and the export returns per unit of product will tend to remain low as the supply of unskilled labour is almost unlimited.

The advice—and assistance—which the poor countries receive from the rich is even nowadays often directed towards increasing their production of primary goods for export. The advice is certainly given in good faith, and it may even be rational from the short term point of view of each underdeveloped country seen in isolation. Under a broader perspective and from a long term point of view, what would be rational is above all to increase productivity, incomes and living standards in the larger agricultural subsistence sectors, so as to raise the supply price of labour, and in manufacturing industry. This would engender economic development and raise incomes *per capita*. But trade by itself does not lead to such a development; it rather tends to have Backsetting Effects and to strengthen the forces maintaining stagnation or regression. Economic development has to be brought about by policy interferences which, however, are not under our purview at this stage of the argument when we are analysing only the effects of the play of the market forces.

Neither can the capital movements be relied upon to counteract international inequalities between the countries which are here in question.

Under the circumstances described, capital will, on the whole, shun the underdeveloped countries, particularly as the advanced countries themselves are rapidly developing further and can offer their owners of capital both good profits and security.

There has, in fact, never been much of a capital movement to the countries which today we call underdeveloped, even in earlier times—except tiny streams to the economic enclaves, mainly devoted to export production of primary products which, however, usually were so profitable to their owners that they rapidly became self-supporting so far as investment capital was concerned and, in addition, the considerably larger but still relatively small investments in railways and other public utilities which had their security in the political controls held by colonial governments. The bulk of European overseas capital exports went to the settlements in the free spaces in the temperate zones which were becoming populated by emigration from Europe. After the collapse of the international capital market in the early 'thirties, which has not been remedied, and later the breakdown of the colonial system. which had given security to the foreign investor, it would be almost against nature if capital in large quantities were voluntarily to seek its way to underdeveloped countries in order to play a role in their economic development.

True, capital in these countries is scarce. But the need for it does not represent an effective demand in the capital market. Rather, if there were no exchange controls and if, at the same time, there were no elements in their national development policies securing high profits for capital—i.e., if the forces in the capital market were given unhampered play—capitalists in underdeveloped countries would be exporting their capital. Even with such controls and policies in existence, there is actually a steady capital flight going on from underdeveloped countries, which in a realistic analysis should be counted against what there is of capital inflow to these countries.

Labour migration, finally, can safely be counted out as factor of importance for international economic adjustment as between underdeveloped and developed countries. The population pressure in most underdeveloped countries implies, of course, that they do not need immigration and the consequent low wages that immigrants are not tempted to come. Emigration from these countries would instead be the natural thing. For various reasons emigration could, however, not be much of a real aid to economic development, even if it were possible.

And the whole world is since the First World War gradually settling down to a situation where immigrants are not welcomed almost anywhere from wherever they come; people have pretty well to stay in the country where they are born, except for touristing by those who can afford it. And so far as the larger part of the underdeveloped world is concerned, where people are "coloured" according to the definition in the advanced countries, emigration is usually stopped altogether by the colour bar as defined by the legislation, or in the administration, of the countries which are white-dominated and at the same time better off economically.

If left unregulated, international trade and capital investments would thus often be the media through which the economic progress in the advanced countries would have Backsetting Effects in the underdeveloped world, and their mode of operation would be very much the same as it is in the circular cumulation of causes in the development process within a single country . . . Internationally, these effects will, however, dominate the outcome much more, as the countervailing Spread Effects of expansionary momentum are so very much weaker. Differences in legislation, administration and *mores* generally, in language, in basic valuations and beliefs, in levels of living, production capacities and facilities, etc., make the national boundaries effective barriers to the spread to a degree which no demarcation lines within one country approach.

Even more important as impediments to the Spread Effects of expansionary momentum from abroad than the boundaries and everything they stand for is, however, the very fact of great poverty and weak Spread Effects within the underdeveloped countries themselves. Where, for instance, international trade and shipping actually does transform the immediate surroundings of a port to a centre of economic expansion, which happens almost everywhere in the world, the expansionary momentum usually does not spread out to other regions of the country, which tend to remain backward if the forces in the markets are left free to take their course. Basically, the weak Spread Effects as between countries are thus for the larger part only a reflection of the weak Spread Effects within the underdeveloped countries themselves.

Under these circumstances the forces in the markets will in a cumulative way tend to cause ever greater international inequalities between countries as to their level of economic development and average national income *per capita.*

* * *

The underdeveloped countries are thus thrown back upon their own resources. They have one asset, the national state, and the possibility it implies of regulating their own economy. To speak in Hegelian terms: *the road to international integration must go over national integration; nationalistic policies by the poor countries and an increase of their bargaining power, won through these policies and through increased cooperation between them as a group, is a necessary stage towards a more effective world-wide international cooperation.*

* * *

The underdeveloped countries in their drive for economic development are in almost all respects up to very much greater difficulties than the now developed countries ever faced. The economic level where they start is in most cases very much lower; the relation between population and resources usually much more unfavourable and the population trends more dynamic and dangerous; they do not have at their disposal an international capital market as the now developed countries had in their time, nor the emigration outlets; they have not inherited the traditions of rationality and the rule of law which were so important in the earlier history of the now developed countries. And they are late-comers; they have not the opportunity, as the now developed countries had, to advance as industrial islands in a surrounding world of backward nations which they could exploit as markets for manufactured goods and as sources of raw materials and for this purpose even keep in colonial bondage. The one advantage they have is our accumulated scientific and technical knowledge.

But to utilise this knowledge they need—and this will be my last point—fresh research in all fields. Neither our techniques of politics, administration and social reforms, nor our techniques in production and distribution can with advantage be simply taken over. As they have developed to suit the conditions of the advanced countries, which are very different, they are not adequate to the needs in underdeveloped countries. Ideally *the underdeveloped countries should utilise all the available knowledge but work out their own specific techniques to fit their values and their actual conditions.* And to do this effectively, they would need to carry on research on all levels, also fundamental research.

They have also for free use our economic theories. But again they should not accept them uncritically but remould them to fit their problems and their interests. They should be aware of the fact that very much of these theories are partly rationalisations of the dominant interests in the advanced and rapidly progressing industrial countries. A very large portion of the literature on the development of underdeveloped countries produced in the advanced countries, for instance, has not had as its value premises our old Western ideals of liberty, equality of opportunities, and common human brotherhood—ideals which are now victoriously conquering the world and which the underdeveloped countries have in common with us—but much narrower national political interests as they are viewed in those advanced countries. This situation has been much worsened under the impact of the cold war when often these national interests even became narrowed down to strategic interests in that world conflict.

More generally speaking, it would be pathetic if the young social scientists in the underdeveloped countries got caught in the predilections of the thinking in the advanced countries, which are hampering the scholars there in their efforts to be rational but would be almost deadening to the intellectual strivings of those in the underdeveloped countries. I would instead wish them to have the courage to throw away large structures of meaningless, irrelevant and sometimes blatantly inadequate doctrines and theoretical approaches and to start out on fresh thinking right from their needs and their problems. This would then take them far beyond the realm of both outmoded Western liberal economics and Marxism.

INTERNATIONAL TRADE AND ECONOMIC DEVELOPMENT

Gottfried Haberler

In another series of Cairo lectures, Professor Gottfried Haberler of Harvard University, a distinguished authority on the theory of international trade, takes strong exception to Gunnar Myrdal's views. He sets forth the arguments, in his opinion conclusive, for believing that international trade must play an important part in the growth of underdeveloped countries.

I shall now positively and systematically state what I think the contribution of international trade to economic development was in the past and what it can be in the future. My overall conclusion is that international trade has made a tremendous contribution to the development of less-developed countries in the nineteenth and twentieth centuries and can be expected to make an equally big contribution in the future, if it is allowed to proceed freely. It does not necessarily follow that a 100 per cent free trade policy is always most conducive to most rapid development. Marginal interferences with the free flow of trade, if properly selected, may speed up development. But I do not want to leave any doubt that my conclusion is that substantially free trade with marginal, insubstantial corrections and deviations, is the best policy from the point of view of economic development. Drastic deviations from free trade can be justified, on development grounds,—and this is very nearly the same thing as to say on economic grounds—only if and when they are needed to compensate for the adverse influence of other policies inimical to economic development, for example, the consequences of persistent inflation or of certain tax and domestic price support policies. Let me guard against a possible misunderstanding. If I say that drastic interferences

Gottfried Haberler, "International Trade and Economic Development," *National Bank of Egypt Fiftieth Anniversary Commemoration Lectures* (Cairo: National Bank of Egypt, 1959). Reprinted by permission of the National Bank of Egypt and Gottfried Haberler.

with the market mechanism are not needed for rapid development, I refer to trade policy and I do not deny that drastic measures in other areas, let me say, land reform, education, forced investment (if the projects are well chosen) etc., may not speed up growth. But I shall in these lectures not further elaborate on those matters.[1]

I shall make use of the so-called classical theory of international trade in its neoclassical form associated with the name of Jacob Viner, James Meade, and Bertil Ohlin, to mention only a few. I shall not try to modernize the theory more than, say, Ohlin and Meade have done, although I shall make an attempt to spell out in some detail the implications of classical trade theory for economic development, an aspect which has perhaps been somewhat neglected. On the other hand, I shall, of course, avoid using the caricature of the theory which is often presented as a portrait by its critics.

Later I shall then take up in detail objections to the orthodox conclusions and shall consider alternative or rival theories put forward by the critics of the orthodox theory.

Let us then start with first things first. International division of labor and international trade, which enable every country to specialize and to export those things that it can produce cheaper in exchange for what others can provide at a lower cost, have been and still are one of the basic factors promoting economic well-being and increasing national income of every participating country. Moreover, what is good for the national income and the standard of living is, at least potentially, also good for economic development; for the greater the volume of output the greater can be the rate of growth—provided the people individually or collectively have the urge to save and to invest and economically to develop. The higher the level of output, the easier it is to escape the "vicious circle of poverty" and to "take off into self sustained growth" to use the jargon of modern development theory. Hence, if trade raises the level of income, it also promotes economic development.

All this holds for highly developed countries as well as for less developed ones. Let us not forget that countries in the former category, too, develop and grow, some of them—not all—even faster than some—not all—in the second category.

In most underdeveloped countries international trade plays quantita-

[1] It also goes without saying that in countries where the Government runs the economy—in the communist countries—it has also to conduct foreign trade. But socialist state trading, if it is efficient and rational and motivated by economic objectives, would be along the lines of comparative cost. I might add that socialist theoreticians fully agree to that, although many do deny that trade in capitalist countries is, in fact, conducted along these lines.

tively an especially important role, that is, a larger percentage of their income is spent on imports, and a larger percentage of their output is being exported, than in the case of developed countries of comparable economic size. (Other things being equal, it is natural that the "larger," economically speaking, a country, the smaller its trade percentages.) Many underdeveloped countries are highly specialized also in the sense that a very large percentage of their exports consists of one or two staple commodities. . . .

This high concentration of exports is not without danger. One would normally not want to put so many of one's eggs into one basket. But the price of diversification is in most cases extremely high. I shall touch on that topic once more. At this point, let me simply say that a high level of concentrated trade will, in most cases, be much better than a low level of diversified trade. How much poorer would Brazil be without coffee, Venezuela, Iran, and Iraq without oil, Bolivia without tin, Malaya without rubber and tin, Ghana without cocoa, and, I dare say, Egypt without cotton. The really great danger of concentration arises in case of deep and protracted slumps in the industrial countries—slumps of the order of magnitude of the Great Depression in the 1930's. In my opinion, and here I am sure the overwhelming majority of economists in the Western World agrees, the chance that this will happen again is practically nil.

The tremendous importance of trade for the underdeveloped countries (as well as for most developed ones, with the exception of the U.S. and U.S.S.R., which could, if need be, give it up without suffering a catastrophic reduction in their living standard) follows from the classical theory of comparative cost in conjunction with the fact that the comparative differences in cost of production of industrial products and food and raw materials between developed countries and underdeveloped countries are obviously very great, in many cases, in fact, infinite in the sense that countries of either group just could not produce what they buy from the other.[2]

The classical theory has been often criticized on the ground that it is static, that it presents only a timeless "cross-section" view of comparative costs and fails to take into account dynamic elements, that is, the facts of organic growth and development. . . .

Now it is true that the theory of comparative cost is static; it is also true that the economies of most countries are changing and developing

[2] In many cases very expensive and poor substitutes can be produced. There is not much sense in contemplating extreme situations. But if I were pressed to guess, I would say that the developed countries as a group, and a few of them individually, could get along without trade a little easier (although still at a terrific loss) than the underdeveloped countries.

and that the theory should take account of that fact. But it is not true that a static theory, because it is static, is debarred from saying anything useful about a changing and developing economic world. There is such a thing as "comparative statics," that is, a method for dealing with a changing situation by means of a static theory. How much can be done by means of comparative statics (as distinguished from a truly dynamic theory) depends on the type of problem on hand. I contend that the problems of international division of labor and long-run development are such that the method of comparative statics can go a long way towards a satisfactory solution.[3] That does not mean, however, that a dynamic theory would not be very useful. Unfortunately, not much of a truly dynamic theory is available at present. What the critics of the static nature of traditional theory have given us over and above their criticism and methodological pronouncements is very little indeed and thoroughly unsatisfactory. But a well known Burmese economist, H. Myint, has recently reminded us that the classical economists, especially Adam Smith and J. S. Mill, were by no means oblivious of the indirect, dynamic benefits which less developed countries in particular can derive from international trade. Going beyond the purely static theory of comparative cost, they have analyzed the "indirect effects" of trade (as J. S. Mill calls them) and thereby presented us with at least the rudiments of a dynamic theory, which Myint aptly calls the "productivity" theory of international trade.[4] Let us then enquire how we can deal by means of

[3] The short run business cycle, on the other hand, is a type of problem of which a static explanation is rather useless. That is the reason why the *static* Keynesian system is so barren. In the short run, dynamic factors completely overshadow and distort the static Keynesian relationships—especially the liquidity preference and the investment function. Needless to add there are plenty of so-called "Keynesian type" dynamic models. But logically they have very little to do with the static Keynesian theory and nothing at all with the chapter on the "Trade Cycle" in *The General Theory*. This type of model building has been launched independently of Keynes by Frisch, Tinbergen and Lundberg. But nobody would deny that many others who later became active in that field thought they were merely dynamizing Keynes.

[4] H. Myint. "The 'Classical Theory' of International Trade and the Underdeveloped Countries," *Economic Journal*, June 1958, pp. 317-337. A. Smith, *Wealth of Nations*, Vol. 1, Cannan ed., p. 413. J.S. Mill, *Principles*, Ashley ed., p. 581. Myint distinguishes from the dynamic "productivity" theory, the "vent-of-surplus" theory and distinguishes the latter also from the static comparative cost theory. This distinction I find unconvincing. The "vent-of-surplus" (if it is not part and parcel of the productivity theory) seems to me simply an extreme case of differences in comparative cost—a country exporting things for which it has no use. This case does not call, it seems to me, for a special theory. But Myint is, of course, quite right that if this extreme situation exists (in modern parlance it might be described as disguised unemployment in export industries) it makes trade appear doubly productive and desirable.

the theoretical tools on hand with the problems of change and development. The tools on hand are the static theory of comparative cost and the semi-dynamic "productivity" theory.

For our purposes I will distinguish among the changes which constitute economic development two types—those that take place independently of international trade and those that are induced by trade or trade policy.

As far as the first group—let me call them autonomous changes—is concerned, I can see no difficulty resulting from them for the applicability of the classical theory of comparative cost. Such changes are the gradual improvement in skill, education and training of workers, farmers, engineers, entrepreneurs; improvements resulting from inventions and discoveries and from the accumulation of capital—changes which in the Western World stem for the most part from the initiative of individuals and private associations, but possibly also from conscious Government policies.[5]

These changes come gradually or in waves and result in gradually increasing output of commodities that had been produced before or in the setting up of the production of goods that had not been produced earlier. Analytically, such development has to be pictured as an outward movement of the production possibility curve (often called substitution or transformation curve). Depending on the concrete turn that autonomous development (including improvements in transportation technology) takes, the comparative cost situation and hence volume and composition of trade will be more or less profoundly affected. But since these changes only come slowly and gradually and usually cannot be foreseen (either by private business or Government planners) in sufficient detail to make anticipatory action possible, there is no presumption that the allocative mechanism as described in the theory of comparative cost will not automatically and efficiently bring about the changes and adjustment in the volume and structure of trade called for by autonomous development.

I turn now to the second type of changes in the productive capabilities of a country which are more important for the purposes of my lectures, namely, those induced by trade and changes in trade including changes in trade brought about by trade policy. Favorable as well as unfavorable trade-induced changes are possible and have to be considered. Alleged unfavorable trade-induced changes have received so much attention from protectionist writers from List to Myrdal (which

[5] I am not speaking here of policies concerning international trade such as the imposition of import restrictions. Changes resulting from trade policy measures are trade induced and not autonomous changes.

has induced free trade economists, too, to discuss them at great length), that there is danger that the tremendously important favorable influences be unduly neglected. Let me, therefore, discuss the latter first.

If we were to estimate the contribution of international trade to economic development, especially of the underdeveloped countries, solely by the static gains from trade in any given year on the usual assumption of given[6] production capabilities (analytically under the assumption of given production functions or given or autonomously shifting production possibility curves) we would indeed grossly underrate the importance of trade. For over and above the direct static gains dwelt upon by the traditional theory of comparative cost, trade bestows very important indirect benefits, which also can be described as dynamic benefits, upon the participating countries. Let me emphasize once more that the older classical writers did stress these "indirect benefits" (Mill's own words).[7] Analytically we have to describe these "indirect," "dynamic" benefits from trade as an outward shift (in the northeast direction) of the production possibility curve brought about by a trade-induced movement along the curve.

First, trade provides material means (capital goods, machinery and raw and semifinished materials) indispensable for economic development. Secondly, even more important, trade is the means and vehicle for the dissemination of technological knowledge, the transmission of ideas, for the importation of know-how, skills, managerial talents and entrepreneurship. Thirdly, trade is also the vehicle for the international movement of capital especially from the developed to the underdeveloped countries. Fourthly, free international trade is the best antimonopoly policy and the best guarantee for the maintenance of a healthy degree of free competition.

Let me now make a few explanatory remarks on each of these four points before I try to show how they fit into, and complement, the static theory of comparative advantage.

The first point is so obvious that it does not require much elaboration. Let us recall and remember, however, the tremendous benefits which the underdeveloped countries draw from technological progress in the developed countries through the importation of machinery, transport equipment, vehicles, power generation equipment, road building machinery, medicines, chemicals, and so on. The advantage is, of course, not all on one side. I stress the advantage derived by underdeveloped

[6] This includes autonomously shifting.

[7] In the neo-classical theory they have been somewhat neglected. The reason is perhaps that these factors do not lend themselves well to precise mathematical treatment.

countries (rather than the equally important benefits for the developed countries), because I am concerned in these lectures primarily with the development of the less developed countries.

The composition of the export trade of the developed industrial countries has been changing, as we all know, in the direction of the types of capital goods which I have mentioned away from textiles and other light consumer goods. This shift has been going on for a long time; it is not a recent phenomenon. But it has proceeded rapidly in recent years, and there is no reason to doubt that it will continue.

Secondly, probably even more important than the importation of material goods is the importation of technical know-how, skills, managerial talents, entrepreneurship. This is, of course, especially important for the underdeveloped countries. But the developed countries too benefit greatly from cross-fertilization aided by trade among themselves and the less advanced industrial countries can profit from the superior technical and managerial know-how, etc. of the more advanced ones.

The late-comers and successors in the process of development and industrialization have always had the great advantage that they could learn from the experiences, from the successes as well as from the failures and mistakes of the pioneers and forerunners. In the 19th Century the continental European countries and the U.S. profited greatly from the technological innovation and achievements of the industrial revolution in Great Britain. Later the Japanese proved to be very adept learners and Soviet Russia has shown herself capable of speeding up her own development by "borrowing" (interest free) immense amounts of technological know-how from the West, developing it further and adapting it for her own purposes. This "trade" has been entirely onesided. I know of not a single industrial idea or invention which the West has obtained from the East.[8] Today the underdeveloped countries have a tremendous,

[8] This statement is made on the authority of Prof. John Jewkes of Oxford who has made a close study of sixty major industrial innovations (in the Schumpeterian sense) and comes to the following conclusion: "The cases taken as a whole reveal that no country has a monopoly of inventive power. The outstanding names and groups are widely spread over many industrial countries. One significant exception is that in none of sixty cases studied had contributions been made by Russian workers subsequent to the Revolution. Before that date numerous names of distinguished Russian contributors crop up." J. Jewkes, "The Sources of Invention," *Lloyds Bank Review,* Jan. 1958, p. 23. The book that contains the material on which the quoted article is based was published under the same title by Macmillan, London, 1958. Note that what I say is that no industrial innovations have come from Russia to the West. That does not mean there are not any. Obviously, in the field of military technology they are doing quite well and it would be surprising if they had not made any innovations elsewhere. But they are probably minor compared with Western achievements and at any rate none has come out.

constantly growing, store of technological know-how to draw from. True, simple adoption of methods developed for the conditions of the developed countries is often not possible. But adaptation is surely much easier than first creation.

Trade is the most important vehicle for the transmission of technological know-how. True, it is not the only one. In fact this function of trade is probably somewhat less important now than it was a hundred years ago, because ideas, skills, know-how, travel easier and quicker and cheaper today than in the 19th Century. The market where engineering and management experts can be hired is much better organized than formerly. There is much more competition in this field as well as in the area of material capital equipment. In the early 19th Century Great Britain was the only center from which industrial equipment and know-how could be obtained, and there were all sorts of restrictions on the exportation of both. Today there are a dozen industrial centers in Europe, the U.S., Canada, and Japan, and even Russia and Czechoslovakia all ready to sell machinery as well as engineering advice and know-how.

However, trade is still the most important transmission belt. What J. S. Mill said 100 years ago is still substantially true:

> It is hardly possible to overrate the value in the present low state of human improvement, of placing human beings in contact with persons dissimilar to themselves, and with modes of thought and action unlike those with which they are familiar . . . Such communication has always been, peculiarly in the present age one of the primary sources of progress.[9]

The third indirect benefit of trade which I mentioned was that it also serves as transmission belt for capital. It is true that the amount of capital that an underdeveloped country can obtain from abroad depends in the first place on the ability and willingness of developed countries to lend, which is of course decisively influenced by the internal policies in the borrowing countries. But it stands to reason—and this is the only point I wanted to make at this juncture—that, other things being equal, the larger the volume of trade, the greater will be the volume of foreign capital that can be expected to become available under realistic assumptions. The reason is that with a large volume of trade the transfer of interest and repayments on principal is more easily effected than with a small volume of trade; and it would be clearly unrealistic to expect large capital movements if the chance for transfer of interests and repayments is not good. There is, furthermore, the related fact that it is much easier to get foreign capital for export industries with their built-in solu-

[9] *Principles of Political Economy.*

tion of the retransfer problem than for other types of investments which do not directly and automatically improve the balance of payments. This preference of foreign capital for export industries is regrettable because other types of investment (such as investment in public utilities, railroads, manufacturing industries) may often (not always) be more productive and may make a greater indirect contribution, dollar per dollar, to economic development by providing training to native personnel and in various other ways than export industries which sometimes (by no means always) constitute foreign enclaves in native soil. If the direct and indirect contribution of non-export industries to national income and economic development are in fact greater than those of the export industry, they should be preferred, because their indirect contribution to the balance of payments position will then also be such as to guarantee the possibility of smooth retransfer of principle and interest—*provided* inflationary monetary policies do not upset equilibrium entailing exchange control that then gets in the way of the transfer. But with inflationary monetary policies and exchange control practices as they are in most underdeveloped countries, the preference of foreign capital for export industries is readily understandable and must be reckoned with and foreign capital in export is better than no foreign capital at all.

The fourth way in which trade benefits a country indirectly is by fostering healthy competition and keeping in check inefficient monopolies. The reason why the American economy is more competitive—and more efficient—than most others is probably to be sought more in the great internal free trade area which the U.S. enjoys rather than in the antimonopoly policy which was always much more popular in the U.S. than in Europe or anywhere else. The importance of this factor is confirmed by the fact that many experts believe that the main economic advantages of the European Common Market, towards the realization of which the first steps have just been taken, will flow from freer competition rather than merely from the larger size and larger scale production which it entails.

Increased competition is important also for underdeveloped countries, especially inasmuch as the size of their market is usually small (even if the geographic area is large). A reservation has nevertheless to be made. The first introduction of new industries on infant industry grounds may justify the creation of monopolistic positions, depending on the size of the country and the type of industry. But the problem will always remain how to prevent the permanent establishment of inefficient exploitative monopolies even after an industry has taken root and has become able to hold its ground without the crutches of import restriction.

The general conclusion, then, is that international trade, in addition to the static gains resulting from the division of labor with given (or autonomously changing) production functions, powerfully contributes, in the four ways indicated, to the development of the productive capabilities of the less developed countries. Analytically we have to express that, in the framework of modern trade theory, by saying that trade gradually transforms existing production functions; in other words, that a movement along the production possibility curves in accordance with the preexisting comparative cost situation, will tend to push up and out the production possibility curve.

ASSISTING ECONOMIC DEVELOPMENT THROUGH PRIVATE INVESTMENT

The White House Conference on International Cooperation

Private investment, both in the form of direct investment in plant and equipment, and portfolio purchases of bonds, was the dominant form of capital transfer from rich to poor countries before World War II. This particular form of "assistance," motivated by economic self-interest, offers certain obvious potential advantages over government-to-government foreign aid. However, the volume of private investment in underdeveloped countries has been modest in recent years. In this report, a group of American experts proposes methods of increasing the role of both domestic and foreign private investment in the economic development process.

PRIVATE INVESTMENT

Private American organizations such as business firms, labor unions, cooperatives, voluntary organizations, foundations, and non-profit enterprises bring a wide variety of advantages to the task of assisting developing nations. Their own special resources, whether capital or skills, are valuable contributions. Many of these organizations can operate with great flexibility and ingenuity. Many have long-standing relationships with private organizations elsewhere in the world.

Equally important is the fact that the voluntary nature of most of these organizations serves as an object lesson to the peoples of the devel-

The White House Conference on International Cooperation, "Assisting Economic Development through Private Investment," (Washington, D.C., December, 1965), in *Blueprint for Peace,* ed. Richard N. Gardner (New York: McGraw-Hill Book Company, 1966), pp. 173-82. The committee that wrote this report included Philip Klutznick (Chairman), Oscar Cox, D. M. Kennedy, Forrest D. Murden, Jr., Robert R. Nathan, Waldemar A. Nielsen, Earl D. Osborn, Frazar B. Wilde, Erwin Schuller, and Andrew Rice.

oping countries, demonstrating to them the value and viability of free institutions. Just as private organizations, with their independence of means and relative freedom for responsible decisions, ensure a pluralistic social order in the United States, so they can encourage other peoples to create independent institutions which will promote the values of human dignity, freedom, and social responsibility.

Another advantage of private assistance activities should be stressed. To the extent that private organizations increase the number of American citizens who are directly or indirectly associated with development work —whether as overseas representatives or loyal supporters back home— a greater understanding of the goals and difficulties of international development is engendered throughout the United States.

Already a large number of private American organizations are engaged in development work, some of it supported by the Agency for International Development and some by independent means. Enormous opportunity remains, however, for increasing the active participation of these and of other non-engaged organizations in the challenging effort of assisting the developing nations.

American business organizations have access to many resources which the developing countries desperately need, not the least of which is a large amount of relatively mobile capital for investment. The entrepreneurial, managerial, and certain technical skills needed by developing nations can often be found only in the private sector of the U.S. economy.

Private enterprise, moreover, can help greatly to establish the kind of network of effective, decentralized decision-makers within an economy that ensures a multiplicity of independent initiatives in the task of economic development. Historically, such decentralized decision-making has characterized every society which has managed to achieve rapid economic growth while preserving both human freedom and social stability.

The need of the developing countries for increased inputs of capital, skills, and energy is so great today that public assistance cannot be supplied in adequate amounts. Private investment remains the only source, a source largely untapped even in recent years, in spite of attempts by the developing nations and most multinational assistance organizations to stimulate the investment flow through an array of promotional services, special credits, guarantees, tax inducements, and other devices.

The accumulated U.S. direct investment of over $15 billion, combined with the substantial investment of other industrialized countries, accounts for one-tenth of the total production of all developing countries today (largely concentrated in the extraction of oil and minerals). But much more needs to be done. Net new American private direct investment (other than in oil) in all of Asia, Africa, and the Middle East in 1963 was substantially less than that in shopping centers in only *one* of the dormitory counties near Washington, DC., in the same year!

Why have only a few hundred U.S. private firms—and correspondingly few firms from other industrialized countries—been playing an active role in development activities abroad?

The answer is clear enough. The primary obligation of the managers of private firms is to be prudent trustees of their stockholders' money. Before making any investment, the managers must make a careful calculation in which potential profits are weighed against risks and difficulties as well as against alternative investment opportunities at home and in other industrialized or developing countries. To date, even with special assistance and inducements, this calculus has dictated against investment in the developing countries by all but a small proportion of the American and European firms which could play a valuable role in economic development. A different pattern of decisions will require major changes in the factors involved in the profit-risk equation.

* * *

However, foreign investment activities, important as they are, can never be expected to cover more than a few major industrial and commercial activities in any developing country. Local enterprises must be relied upon to develop the great number of small and medium-sized businesses which are the bulwark of a modern economy. But even taken together, foreign private investment and domestic private enterprise are making only a small contribution to economic development when judged either by their potential or by the size of the need.

The complex problems of stimulating increased private enterprise activity in developing countries have been intensively studied by many responsible individuals and groups during the past dozen years. After examining earlier studies and proposals, we believe that the heightened need to stimulate foreign private investment today justified serious consideration of somewhat more radical approaches to the problem than other groups have felt able to endorse in the past.

Improving the Investment Climate

The extent of private investment in any developing country will depend, more than anything else, upon the attractiveness of that country's general investment climate. Shaped initially by the country's political and economic ideologies, that climate involves, among many other factors, the legal and administrative rules which circumscribe a private investor and the competence and honesty of local government officials who deal with him.

* * *

Encouraging Local Private Enterprise

While many foreign assistance organizations have undertaken programs designed to encourage the development of local private enterprise, the following steps could improve current activities:

1. The existing complex of development banks, industrial development centers, other local financial institutions in support of private and cooperative enterprises should be substantially assisted to assure that they have the proper direction, staffing, and financing to be effective promoters of local enterprise. The expertise of the United States and other industrialized countries as well as that of other developing countries whose institutions may be relevant should be used.
2. In view of the special need for stronger local banking services in many developing countries, the Agency for International Development should encourage commercial banks to expand their joint venture operations with local commercial banks in developing countries.
3. Multilateral agencies should try to devise workable investment guarantee or insurance programs to protect foreign private investors against political risks.
4. Educational programs designed to develop local managerial and other business skills should be expanded.
5. Private business organizations should increase their efforts to furnish entrepreneurial, managerial, and technical skills to local private enterprise through arrangements such as the International Executive Service Corps.
6. Special programs to identify and support local entrepreneurs in the developing countries should be organized and encouraged.

Mobilizing the Resources of the Financial Community

Before World War II, the investment banking community had long been the major mechanism for mobilizing capital for development purposes, both public and private, in industrialized as well as developing countries. Together with its access to capital, the community possessed unique skills for the formulation of "bankable" projects. For many reasons, however, this traditional role has shifted during the past two decades to multilateral and bilateral government agencies.

Today there are substantial arguments for restoring the private investment banking community to a more influential position in future development financing activities. Private financing is highly flexible in nature. Private bankers, for example, can switch from one payments surplus country to another in search of funds with more flexibility than public authorities can accomplish resource shifts through international negotiations. The many public financial international organizations and arrangements, including the International Monetary Fund and various assistance programs, reduce the risk for private capital venturing into the developing countries by promising a more stable and progressive world economic order.

In view of these considerations, we believe the time has come to reexamine the potential contribution of the world investment banking community, both in its capital and its skills, to development financing. We recommend that:

1. The Agency for International Development experiment with contractual agreements with investment banking organizations to investigate, analyze, and document projects in developing countries which are suitable for private or mixed public-private financing.

2. AID explore the feasibility of making its specific risk guarantees available to American buyers of selected new issues of foreign private enterprises, preferably through underwriters.

3. AID, working closely with the Treasury Department and the investment banking community, explore new devices for using its appropriated funds to obtain a multiplier effect in increasing private capital inputs to developing countries.

Encouraging More Direct Investment

Since direct investment from private sources is an ideal vehicle for the simultaneous input of capital, skills, and energies into developing countries, efforts ought to be made to improve the awareness of investors of specific investment opportunities, to improve the profit-risk ratio affecting such opportunities, and to provide a wider range of private-government risk-sharing arrangements.

We recommend that:

1. United States, multinational, and host country agencies collect and systematize much more accurate information about specific investment opportunities than is now available.

2. The Congress enact a proposal for a tax credit equal to a substantial percentage of the investment by United States investors in productive

facilities in developing countries, to be applied against the total United States tax liability of such investors.

3. The feasibility of special arrangements, similar to those of the domestic Small Business Investment Corporations, should be considered by which international investment corporations could be created for operations in developing countries.

4. The U.S. Government should explore the idea of participating with American operating firms in major industrialization projects, when profit potentials are unknown or doubtful but the project is of great importance, by providing a substantial portion of the capital required in the form of advances, junior to debt, to be repaid only if the operation is successful.

Involving Private Operating Firms without Investment

Some important industrial and commercial projects in the developing countries simply will not attract private direct investment under any conditions. Yet if the justification is great enough, a competent operating firm certainly can provide the best source of technical and managerial skills to develop and operate the project effectively. The technique of the cost-plus-incentive-fee contract, now widely used in the United States for operations in the defense, space and anti-poverty programs, appears to have potential adaptability to those special situations where operating skills are needed but investment prospects are nil. This technique has rarely been used in assistance programs to aid industry and commerce.

We recommend that:

1. AID should be authorized to bring American operating and systems firms into high-priority development projects, where normal private investment is not forthcoming, on a cost-plus-incentive-fee contract basis, possibly with an equity option. Initial equity ownership of such projects normally would be vested in a government corporation or development bank in the developing country involved, but provision should be made to transfer ownership to local and United States private investors at the earliest feasible time. Provision should also be made to train local personnel to replace Americans as rapidly as possible.

2. Other national and multinational aid agencies should be encouraged to provide for similar "chosen instrument" arrangements whenever appropriate.

Enlisting Business Leaders as Advisors to AID

Historically, private businessmen have been the major moving force in the economic development of the United States and other industrialized countries. In contrast, government has been more predominant since World War II in assisting economic development abroad. The role of the business community has been random and sporadic, often consisting of participation by business leaders in temporary advisory, study, or evaluation groups, or of service abroad by individual businessmen within government organizations.

We believe that the time is ripe to arrange for orderly high-level participation of the American business community in our foreign assistance programs. If carefully planned, such an approach could help focus attention upon specific investment oportunities and could stimulate individual firms to join in development efforts abroad.

We recommend that:

1. A permanent International Private Investment Development Board be established consisting of a small number of leading American businessmen who would be given extensive advisory responsibilities within the United States foreign assistance program.

2. Other industrialized countries should be encouraged to establish similar arrangements for responsible business participation in overseas development planning and operations.

As we envision the Board, its members would serve full or parttime and be supported by a small staff. They should have funds for international travel and for contracting with consulting and service organizations when necessary.

Among its advisory responsibilities, the Board would seek to identify development situations where private enterprise could play a special role and try to involve specific U.S. firms in these situations. The Board would investigate high-priority development projects to which private firms had not responded and recommend such government support as believed necessary to insure their participation. In instances when this level of support was approved by the AID Administrator, the Board would act as the agent of AID in arranging for participation of a responsible firm or of a special private consortium.

PART IV

The Challenge of the Poor Nations: The Policy Arena

TOWARD A NEW TRADE POLICY FOR DEVELOPMENT

Raúl Prebisch

Raúl Prebisch, Secretary General of the United Nations Conference on Trade and Development (UNCTAD) from 1964 to 1969, and its leading ideologist, has set forth in his initial report to the Conference a blueprint for reorganizing world trade in the interests of more rapid growth of the underdeveloped countries. This excerpt from his report gives a summary of his views, which were later embodied in the Final Act of the first Conference. Mr. Prebisch, a distinguished Argentinian economist and the intellectual leader of the attack on received doctrines of international trade theory, has been effectively challenged by other economic theorists. However, his views remain, whatever their theoretical virtues or defects, among the most stimulating intellectual contributions to this field.

In this selection, he begins by enumerating the international obstacles to the development of poor countries, and stresses the urgency of reducing the "trade gap," that in his view seriously handicaps the economic development of the underdeveloped countries.

He then goes on to enumerate the responsibilities of the poor countries themselves in speeding up their own development. Finally, he offers proposals for action to stimulate development, composed of four major measures and a number of lesser ones. The major proposals are:

1. *Duty-free entry for the manufactured products of the underdeveloped countries in the markets of rich countries*

Raúl Prebisch, *Toward a New Trade Policy for Development*, excerpts reprinted from *Proceedings of the United Nations Conference on Trade and Development* (New York, 1964), Vol. II, 3-64. Reprinted by permission of the United Nations.

2. Commodity agreements designed to raise and stabilize the prices of poor countries' food and raw material exports
3. Supplementary finance (referred to by Mr. Prebisch in this selection as compensatory finance) which would provide international subsidy for countries whose effective export earnings lag, thereby prejudicing their economic development
4. Economic integration among underdeveloped countries in order to expand their markets and establish industrial production on a more rational basis

As noted above, the first UNCTAD Conference, held at Geneva in 1964, endorsed Mr. Prebisch's platform. However, during the period between the first Conference and the second UNCTAD session (convened at New Delhi in February, 1968), there was very little progress in moving these proposals from resolution to action. It was the hope of the underdeveloped countries at New Delhi that the rich countries would agree to implement at least some elements of the UNCTAD platform, particularly preferential treatment for Southern manufactured exports.

A. EXTERNAL BOTTLENECKS OBSTRUCTING DEVELOPMENT

There is one dominant note in this report. On the international economic scene we are faced with new problems, new in kind, in some cases, and new because of the magnitude they have acquired, in others. We therefore need different attitudes from those prevailing in the past, and these attitudes should converge towards a new trade policy for economic development.

The problems that beset the developing countries are very grave indeed. They have to assimilate modern techniques swiftly in order to raise their levels of living. But new techniques, while they bring enormous advantages with them, are fraught with dangerous consequences, because we have not yet learnt fully to control the forces of development in a rational way.

The direct and indirect effects of technological progress are responsible for the fact that world demand for primary commodities is growing so slowly, to the detriment of the developing countries. The effects of the protectionism prevailing in the industrial countries are an added factor. Even though access to the markets of the latter countries is facilitated, the primary production of the developing countries should adjust to this slow tempo of demand, but structural difficulties prevent it from doing so to the extent necessary to prevent primary commodity prices from deteriorating in relation to those of manufactures. The further modern techniques permeate primary production, the stronger may be the tendency towards such a deterioration. Action by Governments is therefore imperative to deal with this paradox of development.

Such action is also essential for rapid industrialization to become the dynamic factor in the development of the world periphery, just as primary exports were the dynamic factor in the development of the world periphery in former times. But in those days development had no social depth. Today it must. This makes the problem of development more complex and pressing.

The circumstances in which industrialization must proceed are, moreover, very adverse. The developing countries are still suffering the consequences of the disintegration of the world economy that followed upon the great calamity of the 1930s. They do not export industrial goods, except in very small quantities. Since their primary commodity exports are growing so slowly and their terms of trade tend to deteriorate, they lack the resources necessary to import, on an adequate scale, the goods required for a satisfactory rate of development.

These imports are mostly industrial goods, and only part of them have been or could be produced domestically on an economic basis owing to the smallness of national markets. They must export in order to enlarge these markets. But it is usually difficult to increase exports because costs are high, and costs are high because of the difficulty of realizing economies of scale in the absence of exports. Here too a policy is needed, action by Governments to break this vicious circle by providing reasonable access to the markets of the industrial countries for manufactures from the developing countries, and a decided effort to promote the exports of such manufactures.

The developing countries should also form their own groupings in order to plan and develop their industries in wider markets. In some cases they have only just embarked on this policy and they should be given firm international support in the technical and financial fields, within a more favourable institutional framework than now exists. Such co-operation is needed to help import substitution within the groupings with respect not only to goods but also to services, since maritime transport and insurance, for example, represent very substantial external payments.

Among the growing imports necessary for development, capital goods stand out prominently. Such imports have been financed in part by international financial resources. But, in addition to being inadequate, these resources present a further problem. The burden of servicing them grows heavier and heavier, and in some cases the situation is becoming very critical, again because the exports which must provide the necessary funds for servicing are expanding very slowly and losing their purchasing power, while the demand for imports continues to grow.

All these factors that are so unfavourable to the developing countries converge in the persistent trend towards external imbalance that stifles economic development. As was seen at the beginning of this report, it has been estimated that the potential trade gap in goods and services [anticipated exports of goods and services less anticipated imports required to meet economic growth targets] will amount to some $20,000 million by the last year of this decade if the present course of events continues unchecked. This is a staggering figure from the standpoint of the developing countries, but not from that of the industrial countries, since the amount by which the former would have to increase their exports of primary commodities and manufactures in order to bridge this gap, to the extent that it is not covered by international financial resources, represents only an insignificant fraction of the latter's consumption.

The problem must therefore be cut down to its proper size. The remarkable development of the industrial countries has given them a high foreign trade potential. Everything depends on ensuring that part of this potential is translated into practical measures that would bring about a significant increase in imports from the developing countries.

B. THE POTENTIAL OF THE MAJOR INDUSTRIAL COUNTRIES IN RELATION TO DEVELOPMENT REQUIREMENTS

The immediate aim of a new trade policy is to bridge the potential trade gap. Calculations of this gap may serve as a guide for setting targets in the industrial countries for imports of primary commodities and manufactures from the developing countries. But such calculations are only an approximation of the order of magnitude of the phenomenon and therefore give only a general indication of the extent of the changes that may be needed. They cannot be taken as precise, since they are inevitably based on assumptions about the future that the facts may belie. For example, it has been assumed that the rate of income growth in the industrial private-enterprise countries will be 4.2 per cent per annum. This rate may, however, turn out to be higher. If this happens, the demand for imports from the developing countries may be correspondingly greater and thus reduce the magnitude of the potential gap. Would targets that had been set on the assumption of a larger gap then be meaningless? Would they then have to be readjusted?

1. Rates of Growth in Developed and Developing Countries

This is not, of course, a question of mere statistical readjustment. It is a matter of much more importance. If the industrial countries succeed in stepping up their rates of growth, this will create favourable conditions for a corresponding acceleration in the developing countries. The potential gap is the external limiting factor and, if it is reduced, it will be less difficult for the developing countries to reach and exceed the rate of growth postulated for the Development Decade. But at the same time, the inflow of international resources should be increased and this would be more feasible if the industrial countries grew more quickly.

It is therefore a mistake to think that faster growth in the developed countries would necessarily add further to the disparity between their incomes and those of the developing countries. On the contrary, it would create conditions in which the latter would find it easier to overtake the developed countries in their rate of *per capita* growth, thus gradually lessening the disparity which causes so much anxiety.

Countries that assimilate an existing, although constantly changing, technology can and must attain rates of growth much higher than those recorded by the industrial countries in the past, when this productive technology was taking shape. This helps to explain the high rates of growth of the socialist countries and of Japan and the impressive transformation which those countries have undergone. It also explains the extraordinary growth rates of the countries of Western Europe in recent times when they were engaged in modernizing their industrial and agricultural technology, making up for the lag previously created by adverse circumstances. Thanks to the progress thus achieved, all of the countries mentioned have an import potential which could be utilized on a much greater scale than it is now, for their own benefit as well as that of the developing countries.

2. International Monetary Reserves

This potential is also considerable and could be much greater still in some other important countries that are now experiencing balance-of-payments difficulties which tend to slow down their economic expansion. We cannot ignore the significance of this phenomenon in this report because, as we have already said, the consequences of faster growth in the industrial countries would be of the highest importance for the developing countries.

This balance-of-payments problem actually consists of three distinct, although closely interconnected, problems: the problem of monetary reserves, or strictly speaking, liquidity; the problem of trade policy; and the problem of the world production of gold.

The problem of reserves can be summed up as follows. Whereas from 1950-1962 the value of world imports more than doubled, monetary reserves increased by only 33 per cent. Moreover, the distribution of reserves was very uneven. The shortage, which had hitherto been a feature of the countries of continental Western Europe, was remedied at the expense of the reserves of the United States which, for its part, had previously accumulated an excessive share of the world's gold.

The gold reserves of the United States fell from $26,000 million at the beginning of 1950 to $17,000 million at the end of 1962. In evaluating these totals, account should be taken of the net position of foreign short-term claims upon the United States, which rose from $5,500 million at the beginning of 1950 to $16,900 million by the end of 1962.

These developments were the results of an external deficit which, during this thirteen-year period, reached a total of $25,900 million. The deficit occurred in spite of a large surplus in exports of goods and services. But it so happens that United States loans, investment and grants-in-aid in the rest of the world exceed this export surplus.

The existence in the United States of such a vast quantity of assets belonging to foreign monetary authorities seems to be one of the factors that restrict that country's freedom of action, as regards the measures it can adopt to correct the external imbalance.

Hence emphasis has been laid on restoring liquidity, and solutions are being sought with that purpose in mind. In short, the aim is to add, in one form or another, new resources to those now available in the International Monetary Fund. In certain cases, the thinking goes even further: it is suggested that these operations may be organized in a regular and systematic manner as part of an international mechanism and in a way that relieves the major industrial countries of the burden of holding other countries' monetary reserves and thereby impairing their freedom of action, as mentioned above.

3. *The Trade and Financial Policy of the Key Countries*

These solutions are very important from the point of view of international liquidity, but they are not basic solutions to the problem of imbalance, nor do they claim to be. This brings us to the second problem: trade policy. Until recently major countries of western Europe were accumulating large monetary reserves since their loans, investments and grants-in-aid to the rest of the world were less than their trade surplus. The automatic mechanism has not functioned well or has functioned too slowly.

The basic solution to the problem must be sought both in credit and investment policy and in trade policy. If, in addition to lending and investing more abroad, these countries open their doors wider to imports of primary commodities and industrial products from the developing countries, this would have favourable effects not only for the latter but for the world as a whole in view of the interdependence of world trade. The manpower shortage, which has been a feature of these European countries, could greatly facilitate the implementation of a more liberal trade policy.

It is remarkable that, given such favourable conditions for external payments, one of the most persistent remnants of bilateralism has still not been abandoned: the requirement that resources allocated to the developing countries must be used in the lending country.

4. The Dynamic Role of Gold

Let us now briefly consider the third problem. During the period 1950-1962, visible stocks of gold increased by only 17 per cent while, as has already been said, world trade doubled. Much of the gold produced has gone into private hoards. We are not, of course, saying that there has to be a close link between world trade and monetary reserves, especially if better use could be made of the reserves in solving the problem of liquidity, but there can be no doubt that, if there had been abundant output and less hoarding of gold, the reserves position would be much easier.

Still, this is not the only important aspect of gold; there is another, perhaps even more important from the dynamic point of view. In other days, new production of gold was a significant factor in increasing the demand for exports of goods and services; and this factor has now become weaker. Thus, gold, apart from being the basic element of monetary reserves, has this dynamic role to play. Sometimes it is suggested that gold should be revalued in order to stimulate production and, at the same time, enlarge existing reserves. But the disadvantages of this suggestion are considered to outweigh the advantages. Hence, other solutions must be sought. The possibility is mentioned of creating new international resources on the basis of part of existing reserves, in the same way as central banks create internal resources. These resources would be put at the disposal of existing international credit institutions so they can make loans to the developing countries, in accordance with rules and principles approved by governments. Similarly, it has also been suggested that other forms of reserves should be used in addition to gold.

The time may have come to examine these aspects in the relevant circles. A wise and constructive solution would be very effective in helping to speed up development, not only because of the direct impact that these additional resources would have on the capacity to import of developing countries, but also because of the impetus that these larger imports would give to the economies of the industrial countries and their rates of growth.

5. *Resources from Disarmament*

When one reflects on the need for additional resources for investment, one's mind naturally goes back to the enormous possibilities for releasing resources that would be opened up by world-wide disarmament. The Declaration, which the United Nations adopted in 1953 and in which the Governments of Member States expressed their intention to devote a portion of those resources to economic development "when sufficient progress has been made in internationally supervised world-wide disarmament" is still in effect.

It has been estimated that annual expenditure on armaments amounts to some $120,000 million. In the industrial countries,[1] this represents about 8 to 9 per cent of national income. If 1 per cent of such income became available as a result of disarmament, the allocation of international resources to the developing countries could rise from the present figure of 0.5 per cent of the aggregate income of these industrial countries to 1.5 per cent. This would enable the developing countries, provided an appropriate policy were followed, to raise their annual rate of overall growth to 7 per cent, instead of the 5 per cent established for the Development Decade. If this were to happen, the average *per capita* income of Western Europe could be matched not in eighty years but in almost half that time.

Furthermore, if part of the resources released by disarmament were used to increase the productive investment of the industrial countries, this would give a greater impetus to their own growth and to the demand for imports from the developing countries and help to accelerate the flow of these imports.

[1] Including socialist countries.

C. THE RESPONSIBILITY OF THE DEVELOPING COUNTRIES

While technological progress in the industrial centres and its gradual spread to the rest of the world creates new problems at the international level, as was stated at the beginning of this part of the report, it also creates problems in the developing countries and requires new attitudes and gigantic efforts by the latter countries to solve such problems.

The obstacles in the way of this effort are formidable. In many developing countries, however, attention is often centred on the external obstacles; the problems seem more urgent there, perhaps because they are more conspicuous. But it would be dangerous self-deception to imagine that, once these external obstacles are overcome, the way will be wide open for spontaneous economic development.

On the contrary, the determination to overcome these obstacles and exert a conscious and deliberate influence on the forces of economic and social development is also essential. The policy of international co-operation is only complementary; it cannot be a substitute for internal development policy. Nor can the internal policy fulfil its aims without effective and timely international co-operation.

This report would therefore be incomplete if we failed to remember the nature of the main obstacles to be overcome internally. In every country there is a different complex of problems, and the attitudes towards them are also different; the risks implicit in these generalizations should therefore be borne in mind.

1. *The Internal Changes Required by Development*

Generally speaking, there are three main obstacles in the way of propagating technological advances and which therefore obstruct the growth of productivity and *per capita* income in the developing countries: land tenure; limited social mobility and the ignorance of the masses; and the concentration of income in the hands of relatively small population groups.

The forms of land tenure generally to be found in the developing countries are plainly incompatible with technological progress. This is particularly so, when a large part of the productive land is concentrated in the hands of a few, while a very large number of small and medium-sized holdings generally make up a tiny proportion of the cultivable land. All this conspires to frustrate development; in some cases, because the high rent already received by the landowner makes him reluctant to take the trouble of introducing modern techniques, and, in others, because the very size of the holdings and the shortage of resources for investment are often such that contemporary techniques cannot be fully and properly used.

The ignorance of the masses and limited social mobility are two aspects of the same problem. If up-to-date techniques are to penetrate, there must be opportunities for learning and training and easy access to such opportunities. Conditions must also be favourable for the most able and dynamic people at all social levels to come forward and get ahead. Generally speaking, this happens to a very limited extent only, which means that a vast human potential is wasted, just as the out-dated forms of land tenure impede exploitation of the enormous productive potential of the land.

The concentration of income is, of course, linked to these other two features and, in many cases, is aggravated by the serious effects of inflation, a phenomenon usually also influenced by structural factors. It might be thought that this concentration would actively contribute to capital formation, but this is so only in exceptional cases. More commonly, high incomes means superfluous and excessive consumption by the groups that have them, to the detriment of the investment that technological progress requires on an ever-growing scale.

It would a serious mistake, however, to imagine that the problem of capital formation could be fundamentally solved in most developing countries, if this savings potential of the high-income groups could be used for investment rather than consumption, and if, at the same time, the flight of capital, which reaches rather significant figures in several developing countries, could be avoided. There is no doubt that all this must be done and that the tax instrument should be used together with other measures for the purpose. But in many countries the problem of capital formation has also to be tackled resolutely with international financial resources, which, by stimulating the rapid growth of income, help to create opportunities for domestic capital formation that are now extremely slight.

The weakness of the development impetus in many of the peripheral countries is a result of all these internal factors that combine in a particular social structure, in addition to the external factors that hamper growth. Development calls for changes in the forms of production and in the economic structure which cannot come about unless a change in the social structure leaves the way open to the forces of technological progress.

Without such changes industrialization cannot run its full course. Generally speaking, industrialization has simply superimposed itself on the existing state of affairs without basically altering it. Furthermore, the excessive protectionism frequently sheltering industries adds a further privilege to those already existing in the distribution of income.

Again, industrial development is constricted not only by the lack of exports but also by the smallness of the internal market. Rural masses working generally in a very unproductive way, urban masses who, to a large extent, take refuge in very low-paid artisan occupations and personal services, or who waste their efforts in antiquated forms of trading—these do not provide a large and lively market for the products of industrial development. And industry itself does not generate, to the extent desired, the income that could create its own strong market; for excessive protectionism and restrictions on imports usually shield it from healthy competition and weaken the incentive to raise productivity and the incomes of the people who work in it through the efficient use of men and machines.

2. Industrialization and Demographic Growth

But the problem is not a simple one. The development of the domestic market through technological improvements in agriculture, better marketing organization, the gradual elimination of artisan occupations, and a gradual decrease in the number of people precariously employed in personal services, will release an enormous potential of workers who will swell the ranks of those who, owing to the high rate of population growth, have to be incorporated in the economy each year. It is the extremely important dynamic function of industry and other activities which thrive with it to absorb this human potential at a satisfactory level of productivity. If they are to fulfil this absorptive function effectively, all these activities must forge ahead all the faster as modern techniques penetrate to those strata of the population which are technologically so conspicuously backward.

The nature of this question should be stressed here, for it is still asserted sometimes that the solution of the development problem is to be sought in the domestic market and not in the expansion of exports.

The fact is that the development of the domestic market and the promotion of exports are not two alternative or mutually exclusive propositions. The two processes must take place simultaneously and in a coordinated manner. The penetration of modern techniques to the submerged strata of the population is an inevitable prerequisite for accelerating growth. If this acceleration is to be achieved, the persistent trend towards external imbalance must be overcome through the expansion of exports and other measures of international economic co-operation.

This dynamic role of industry and other activities in the absorption of the human potential is a key element in the process of development. In most cases, this role is not being played well. For example, in Latin America the minimum rate of *per capita* income growth of 2.5 per cent a year, laid down as a target in the Punta del Este Charter, would not be sufficient to bring about this absorption under the present conditions in which modern techniques are penetrating rather slowly. If the penetration could be speeded up, it would become even more imperative to expedite growth and industrialization.

Naturally, when the subject of accelerating development is broached, the question is often asked whether the developing countries could not themselves attain this objective by lowering their rates of demographic growth.

There would seem, however, to be very little prospect of achieving such a reduction in the next decade. Historically, the decline in the birth rate has been a consequence of industrialization and of improvement in the level of living, and this process has been very gradual. On the other hand, it is difficult to envisage the possibility of bringing about a sharp reduction in the birth rate quickly by a conscious and deliberate policy. It has been pointed out more than once that, even where religious considerations do not affect the implementation of such a policy, it would encounter formidable social, educational and economic difficulties. The success that might be achieved is therefore very uncertain. Actually, with the leeway which the developing countries still have to make up in order to reduce their death rates, and with persons of marriageable age forming an increasing proportion of their populations, the rate of demographic growth appears more likely to rise than to fall in the immediate future.

Be that as it may, reducing the rate of population growth cannot in any sense be an alternative to the vigorous development policy advocated in this report. It could not be a method of evading or slackening the effort which this policy necessarily entails; on the contrary, it would be a means of deriving more far-reaching and effective results from such a policy.

3. *Development Planning and International Co-operation*

All these considerations give us some idea of the nature and complexity of the changes which development demands. Furthermore, these changes call for a great effort to mobilize resources which, like the changes themselves, need to be given a definite direction and clear economic and social objectives. Hence the need for development planning.

Planning is something more than a new technique superimposed on the framework of public administration, which is usually so defective in the developing countries. Here again, basic changes are required both in thinking and in action, and such changes are far from easy to make.

* * *

In all of this there is a clear convergence of responsibilities, internally as well as internationally. The controversy about whether internal ills are caused by external factors or whether the source of these ills should be sought exclusively in the behaviour of the country concerned has been rendered obsolete by events and is meaningless now. There are both internal and external factors to be attacked simultaneously. To emphasize the former and exclude the latter, or vice versa, would be an aimless exercise and only divert our attention from the real solutions.

D. THE CONCERTING OF TRADE MEASURES

These solutions cannot be adopted in isolation, since they form an integral part of a more comprehensive policy of international co-operation for economic development. Solutions of this kind have been outlined in Part Two of this report, as a basis for discussion rather than as final proposals. It may be helpful for us to recapitulate them briefly here.

1. Import Targets

With regard to primary commodities and industrial goods produced by the developing countries, it is advocated that *quantitative targets* should be set for their entry into the industrial countries' markets, to be reached within a certain number of years.

The import targets for *primary commodities* could be, depending on the individual case, quantities of specific commodities or groups of commodities, or desired proportions of the consumption, or of the increase in consumption, of each importing country.

The targets for *industrial goods* could be expressed for each importing country in terms of a *global value* covering the quota of imports of manufactures enjoying preferences and the minimum target of imports not subject to preferences that should be attained in order to help eliminate the trade gap.

Cases of *injury to domestic producers* resulting from exceptional increases in imports from developing countries should be dealt with under the normal procedures laid down by GATT.

2. *Industrial Preferences*

Within the aforesaid global value, the industrial countries could establish a quota for admitting manufactured goods from the developing countries *free of duty*, but they could *exclude from these preferences* a schedule of items constituting a reasonable percentage of the total goods they import. This exclusion could take effect from the outset or during the operation of the system, in accordance with criteria to be laid down.

Manufactures from developing countries thus excluded from the scope of preferences would be admitted by the industrial countries on the usual most-favoured-nation basis.

All the developing countries, irrespective of their level of development, would be eligible to avail themselves of the *preferential system* up to the amount of the relevant quota. But there would have to be a periodic review of the flow of exports; and if exports from one or more countries increased so much that they did not leave sufficient room for those from the others, equitable solutions should be sought.

Special preferences could be granted to the less advanced developing countries. For this purpose, the list of items excluded by the industrial countries from the preferential system applied to all developing countries should be used.

The preference would *remain in force for ten years* from the time when each industry in a given country started to export. But this period could be extended in accordance with internationally agreed procedures, if an *exception to the rule* was fully justified.

3. *Existing Preferences*

The ultimate objective should be to adapt existing preferential arrangements to the new system of preferences in such a way that there is *no discrimination among developing countries,* and so that developing countries presently obtaining such preferences should continue receiving *benefits* under the new system at least *equivalent* to those they now enjoy. The precise way in which this ultimate objective might be secured is a matter for further discussion but it should include, in particular, international technical and financial assistance to countries at the earliest stage of economic development.

In any case, preferences granted by developing to industrial countries should cease.

4. Nature of the Targets

The targets are an expression of the *objectives to be reached;* thus they are of an indicative character and generally speaking, do not constitute commitments to import. But the targets for primary commodities, in addition to representing quotas of goods to be imported without restrictions, might constitute *commitments to purchase* over a number of years.

When the targets are set, Governments would pledge to take all necessary action to reach them, including *promotional measures in the technical, trade and financial fields.*

In the socialist countries, the targets would also be of an *indicative character*, but they should be translated into long-term commitments to import under the system of bilateral agreements.

5. Commodity Agreements

Two converging kinds of measures are envisaged to *guarantee the purchasing power of exports* of primary commodities: commodity agreements and compensatory financing.

Commodity agreements can be used to establish minimum prices or improve prices, as the case may be, by maintaining their parity with those of manufactures, when the price improvement does not *substantially affect* consumption by reducing it or by giving synthetics and substitutes a competitive advantage.

Commodity agreements should establish whatever system of *export quotas* may be necessary to support the price policy.

When internal prices are higher in the industrial countries than on the international market, the adverse effects on consumption could be avoided if the raising of prices was accompanied by an *equivalent lowering of tariffs or internal taxes* where such exist.

In the case of *tropical commodities,* the internal taxes should be lowered still more until they are completely eliminated, so as to encourage consumption.

As regards competition from *synthetics and substitutes,* there might be cases in which it is advisable to *increase productivity and lower the costs and prices of* some natural commodities, provided that the loss of income thus suffered by the exporting countries is offset through compensatory financing.

Whenever the temporary shortage of a primary commodity leads to price rises that adversely affect producers and consumers, *ceiling prices* should be set. The agreements should also lay down rules for the disposal of surpluses and non-commercial stocks.

The scope of commodity agreements, or of corresponding inter-governmental action, should be considerably extended and conditions should be laid down for access to the markets of the industrial countries through *import quotas* and *import commitments,* where feasible; in addition, provision should be made for the gradual lowering of *support prices* and arrangements made for co-ordinating the internal and external production policy of the importing and exporting countries. The purpose of all these steps is to ensure that the latter obtain a reasonable share in the growth of consumption of the former.

6. Compensatory Financing

Compensatory financing is imperative to the extent that it may not be possible, through commodity agreements, to prevent the exporting countries from suffering losses owing to deterioration in the terms of trade.

Two kinds of losses would have to be compensated *henceforth:* those due to *the previous deterioration in the terms of trade* and those resulting from *future deteriorations.*

The *amount of compensation* to be received by each exporting country would be determined after consideration of the effect that the deterioration has had on its investment resources and balance of payments, so that the country can receive whatever additional resources it needs to continue *its economic development plan* without disturbances.

These *additional resources* should not be transferred directly to producers, except where this is essential to ensure the normal development of production.

Each country should take whatever internal action it sees fit to obtain resources for *compensatory financing.* But it should not do so through taxes which, by raising prices for the consumer, *discourage consumption or encourage the replacement* of natural commodities by substitutes or synthetics.

The compensatory resources might form part of a fund administered by *international credit institutions,* at either the international or the regional level, in accordance with rules approved by Governments.

The required resources might also be made available to developing countries by national and international agencies acting through consortia or by other suitable co-operative arrangements.

In either case, the relevant decisions might be based on an independent finding by an *international team of independent experts* of the highest standing that a particular country's economic development was being prejudiced by terms-of-trade losses.

7. Readjustment of the External Debt

Consideration should be given to the *readjustment of repayment periods* and terms of the *external debt* of some countries. External financing could facilitate this operation. Steps should also be taken to avoid the subsequent recurrence of critical situations resulting from excessive increases in the burden of servicing.

8. Maritime Transport and Insurance

The possibility should be examined of developing merchant marines and insurance operations within regional groupings of developing countries or of promoting among them specialization in the miscellaneous activities that constitute these services.

The system of shipping conferences and the impact of their agreements on the developing countries should also be examined.

9. Groupings of Developing Countries

The developing countries should pursue their industrialization policies and especially their *import substitution* policies and should endeavour to pool their efforts rationally by means of preferential groupings on as large a scale as possible.

These preferential groupings should be supplemented by *payments agreements* between their constituent members.

10. The GATT Rules

The GATT rules now in force should be amended to take into account the consequences of the structural inequalities between industrial and developing countries. These amendments should relate in particular to reciprocity with a view to establishing the concept of *implicit reciprocity;* to the *preferences* granted by the industrial countries to the *developing countries;* and to the *preferences granted by developing countries to each other* through groupings of countries.

11. Reduction of Excessive Tariffs

Without being committed to reciprocity, developing countries with excessive protectionism should undertake *to lower their high tariffs* as they gradually counter the trend towards external imbalance by expanding their exports of primary and industrial products and by import substitution.

12. Differences Between the Developing Countries

In the application of these concerted measures, it is essential to recognize the different situations of the developing countries, depending on the degree of their development, and to adapt and co-ordinate the measures adopted so that the advantages deriving therefrom accrue in particular to the *less advanced of the developing countries* in order to give strong impetus to their growth. In this connexion, not only might the less advanced countries to be given general preferences, shared with the other developing countries irrespective of their degree of development, and special preferences, but they should also receive particular attention so far as the measures for promoting their exports are concerned. They should also be given special attention as regards the allocation of international financial resources; the per capita volume of the resources that these countries obtain should generally be greater than that granted to the more advanced of the developing countries and especially to those of them which may already have improved their ability to generate their own investment resources.

E. NATURE AND ADAPTABILITY OF THE POLICY OF INTERNATIONAL CO-OPERATION

Now that the principal measures proposed in this report have been thus summarized, two important observations should be made.

The first concerns the very nature of the policy which embraces all these measures. It is not simply a matter of lowering or removing barriers which stand in the way of the developing countries' trade and of laying down more appropriate rules than those now in force. What is required is positive action.

This is the significance of the import targets. They are the tangible and practical expression of the responsibility which Governments—both of the industrial and of the developing countries—may decide to assume in order to achieve certain basic foreign trade objectives. And this responsibility would necessarily involve the adoption of whatever measures may be called for, both internal and international.

Thus, should the import targets set be insufficiently high, or prove to be so in practice, the inflow of international finance would have to be increased to cover the trade gap.

This does not mean that import targets and external financial aid are interchangeable concepts. Actually, the quantity of external finance should rather be a supplement to internal investment resources, to compensate for their present scarcity. Under normal circumstances, their direct role should not be to bridge the gap. This has to be done through the expansion of exports. Hence there is no conflict between trade and aid. Each of these has its specific role to play.

Consequently, the extent to which exports and international financial resources have to be co-ordinated is not arbitrary. The proportion of these resources in each country's investment programme must become smaller in the course of time as domestic savings capacity draws strength from the economic development process itself. Exports, on the other hand, must expand continuously in order to cover mounting import requirements and pay for servicing the external debt.

All this points to desirability of periodically examining the way in which those objectives are being achieved, not as ends in themselves but as means which, in combination with others, would make it possible to reach a bigger target, the growth target set for the United Nations Development Decade and the more satisfactory targets which may be established later.

The second observation concerns the flexibility with which this policy must be carried out. The developing countries have certain very important common denominators, but there are also great disparities between them, deriving from their different degrees of development and from the particular problems that affect them. Owing to these disparities, the measures advocated here would also have very different effects from country to country. Thus, while access to the manufactured goods markets of the industrial countries is important for all, some developing countries would be able to enjoy the advantages of these measures much earlier than others, unless those opportunities are accompanied by very energetic promotional measures in the countries which would otherwise lag behind. Commodity agreements or compensatory financing would also have a very diverse impact. All of the foregoing emphasizes the need to bear in mind these disparities in degrees of development and in individual situations. The decisive element here could be international technical and financial aid. The intensity of this aid would have to be geared to those disparities so that all the countries could expedite their pace of growth, or maintain it in the few cases where an acceptable tempo has been attained.

This very heterogeneity opens up interesting vistas so far as the dynamics of development is concerned. At one extreme are the countries which are close to a level of income that will enable them, in a relatively short time, to grow at a satisfactory pace with their own resources, but which have to correct the persistent trend towards external imbalance so they can convert part of these resources into imports of capital and other goods needed for their economic development. At the other extreme are the countries which are only beginning to develop, and there the top priority is to obtain international finance, most especially for building up their generally weak economic infrastructure and for basically important social investments. The countries which are at an incipient stage of development may possibly not have to contend with an acute persistent imbalance as do the former, since this imbalance is a consequence of development; but it would be advisable to act now to prevent this from occurring in the future by guiding their development, and particularly their industrialization policy, along rational lines, both by import substitution within groupings of countries and by the promotion of exports of manufactures.

In the course of time, the more advanced of the developing countries should be able to provide a market for exports of manufactures from countries which are embarking on the first stages of industrialization by according them preferential treatment.

In all of this there is no master plan, drawn up once and for all, that is equally applicable to all countries. That is why this policy is necessarily a complex one. Furthermore, it must respond and adapt itself continually to endless changes.

TRADE PREFERENCES AND DEVELOPING COUNTRIES

Harry G. Johnson

Harry G. Johnson, Professor of Economics at the London School of Economics and the University of Chicago, has made many contributions to monetary theory and to the theory of international trade. In this article, he discusses the arguments for and against trade preferences in the broader setting of the theory of economic growth. This article draws upon Professor Johnson's recent book, Economic Policies Toward Less Developed Countries *(1967).*

The most original new idea on policies to further the economic development of the underdeveloped world—and the most seductive to the developing countries themselves—that emerged from the first United Nations Conference on Trade and Development at Geneva in 1964 was undoubtedly the proposal for temporary trade preferences in industrial products to be granted by the advanced countries.

This proposal, the brain-child of Dr. Raúl Prebisch, Secretary-General of the conference, evoked sharp divisions among the leading industrial nations. The Americans adamantly opposed any consideration of preferential trading schemes.[1] The British indicated a willingness to generalize Commonwealth preferences to all less developed countries, provided that other developed countries would grant similar preferences. The Common Market countries were divided between support of the "Brasseur Plan" for the organization of markets and advocacy of preferential

Harry G. Johnson, "Trade Preferences and Developing Countries," *Lloyds Bank Review,* Vol. LXXX (April, 1966), 1-18. Reprinted by permission of *Lloyds Bank Review* and Harry G. Johnson.

[1] The academic reasoning behind the official American position has been presented with admirable clarity and balance by Professor Gardner Patterson in his article "Would Tariff Preferences Help Economic Development?" in the April, 1965, issue of this *Review.*

arrangements of a "non-discriminatory" character (according to GATT concepts).

The less developed countries themselves were divided in economic interests. For those of them belonging to the British Commonwealth or to the Associated Overseas Territories of the European Economic Community enjoy a preferential advantage in these markets over their rivals in non-member developing countries. A united front in demanding preferences was achieved only by incorporating the proviso that developing countries which lost by the extension of preferences should be adequately compensated.

TRADE AND AID

The primary purpose of the 1964 United Nations Conference on Trade and Development was to consider possibilities for new policies in the field of trade that would, by enlarging the export earnings of the developing countries, help to fill the prospective "foreign-exchange gap" between their growing import and debt-service requirements and the foreign exchange likely to become available from their relatively slower-growing exports and from the virtually stagnant volume of foreign aid from the developed countries. In much of the documentation of UNCTAD, and of the argument at and about the conference, there is a clear basic assumption that "aid" and "trade" are substitutes for one another. This assumption is consonant with the main lines of contemporary thinking on problems of development finance, which takes as its frame of reference the balance-of-payments constraint on policy. But from a more fundamental point of view, one which concentrates on the real resource requirements of economic development, this assumption is not merely superficial but erroneous in important respects.

"Aid," properly defined, entails a transfer of real resources from the aid-giving developed country to the aid-receiving developing country. Such resources have the special attraction to the latter of being immediately usable externally, whereas domestic resources made available by saving and taxation have to be converted into external resources through exporting or import-substitution. The transfer involves a sacrifice by the aid-giving country, and a gain by the aid-receiving country.

This proposition, however, has to be qualified by recognition that what is officially catalogued as "aid" is a heterogeneous mixture of grants, loans and transfers in kind, much of it tied to purchases at prices (or reckoned at notional values) above world market prices. When allowance is made for future repayments of interest and amortization on loans, and for excessive prices of aid-financed goods, the real resource transfers involved in foreign aid today probably run to no more than about half the nominal total.[2]

"Trade," on the other hand, is the provision of better opportunities to sell goods in export markets, goods whose production and export necessitates the expenditure of real resources and whose import provides additional real resources to the importing country. An explicit transfer is involved only if the trade opportunity enables the exporting country to charge, and obliges the importing country to pay, higher prices than would otherwise prevail. Significantly, it was trade opportunities of this kind that were sought in the demands voiced at the 1964 UNTAD conference: for commodity agreements to raise the prices of primary products and for trade preferences in industrial products. If trade preferences had the expected effect of enabling exporters to charge the domestic price of the importing country, instead of the world market price, their effect would be simply to transfer tariff revenue from the government of the importing country to the producers of the exporting country. Expanded trade opportunities may, however, and frequently will, involve only the opportunity to sell more goods at about the same prices as previously prevailed (depending on the circumstances of international competition). In this case, there is no explicit transfer, and the effects have to be evaluated in terms of the theory of the gains from trade.

GAINS FROM TRADE

According to this theory, the exporting country gains to the extent that the goods purchased with the additional export proceeds are worth more than the goods that the resources required to produce the additional exports could have produced in other activities, such as subsistence agriculture or the import-substitution sector of the economy. For developing countries—which typically incur substantial excess costs in substituting for imports—this gain could be substantial. But, obviously, it could never be so great as to equal the value of the additional export proceeds if these were received as a gift. Thus this kind of trade opportunity, which for practical purposes can be identified with non-discriminatory tariff reduction (and some types of preferential trading arrangements), cannot be a substitute for an equivalent flow of aid.

[2] John Pincus (*Economic Aid and International Cost Sharing*, Baltimore, The Johns Hopkins Press, 1965, Chap. 5) estimates that conventional measures of aid overstate its real cost to the donors by 70 to 100 per cent.

For its part, the importing country will gain in real terms if providing the trade opportunity enables it to substitute cheaper imports for more expensive domestic output ("trade-creation"). In this case, expanding the trade opportunities it offered to developing countries would enable it to give more aid without reducing its real income—in contradiction to the notion prevalent among developed countries that the "sacrifice" of more trade would excuse a policy of less aid. On the other hand, the importing country will lose in real terms if providing the trade opportunity involves switching imports to a higher-cost source of supply ("trade diversion"). This possibility of loss arises only with preferential (as opposed to non-discriminatory) tariff reduction; and, given that the tariff rates on which preferences would be based are almost universally less than 100 per cent, the loss involved could be only a fraction of the value of the trade switched.

To sum up, except where "trade" merely raises the prices received by the developing countries for their exports, "trade" and "aid" are *not* substitutes. In particular, "trade" may increase and not reduce the real resources available to the developed country, while "trade" may be substantially less useful than an equal flow of aid to the developing country. This last point, by itself, suggests pessimism with respect to the potential contribution of "trade" to development. Such pessimism, however, is not wholly black, for one must take account of the dynamic (as distinct from the financing) aspects of the development problem, and the possible differences between trade and aid in this respect.

The process of industrialization is not a matter merely of accumulating the capital necessary to establish the capital-to-output ratio required by an industrial economy. It is much more one of inculcating in those who manage and use the capital the habits of seeking constantly to improve efficiency, so that economic growth becomes a self-sustaining process. This is a matter of education and social psychology about which too little is known; however, historical and increasing contemporary evidence suggests that exposure to competition in a large market can play an important part in the process.

Observation of the industrial problems of the developing countries also suggests that, typically, their markets are too small for their efforts at industrialization on the basis of import-substitution to bring this force into play. This implies that "aid," which characteristically—at least until very recently—has been devoted to supporting import-substituting industrialization policies, does little to stimulate the dynamic processes of growth, and may even reinforce the factors that tend to suppress them in small highly-protected economies. "Trade," on the other hand, could evoke dynamic responses to competitive opportunities that would reinforce the growth process, and so be more fruitful in the longer run than aid. This would depend, however, on whether the trade opportunities offered were such as to offer rewards to competitive ability, or merely provided limited monopolistic privileges in a closely controlled market.

IS NON-DISCRIMINATION ECONOMICALLY SENSIBLE?

The principle of non-discrimination is the principle that the same rate of duty should apply to all imported goods, regardless of their country of origin. This principle is the foundation of the GATT system of regulating international trade; and the conviction that the principle represents an ideal for the conduct of international commercial diplomacy underlies much of the aversion with which commercial policy negotiators regard the trade preferences proposal.

As applied within GATT, however, the principle is inherently self-contradictory, owing to the exception allowed to it for free trade areas and customs unions. For this exception converts the principle into the rule that discriminatory tariffs are bad unless they go to the limit of 100 per cent discrimination. More fundamentally—as trade theorists have long been pointing out—non-discrimination between sources of supply of individual goods is by no means the same thing as non-discrimination between countries exporting to a particular national market. Tariff rates may be set high on goods of which one country is the preponderant supplier, and low on goods of which another country is the predominant supplier.

This possibility of discrimination between countries, by appropriate selection of commodities for favourable tariff treatment, has in fact been exploited in past rounds of negotiations under GATT. The negotiation machinery has perforce concentrated on bargaining between the large "dominant-supplier" countries, which can offer profitable access to markets and also benefit from the receipt of tariff concessions. The item-by-item approach has enabled these countries to concentrate tariff reductions on those goods in which they have an important trading interest.

The "dominant-supplier"—authority of the U.S. Trade Expansion Act—since made irrelevant by Britain's failure to secure membership in the Common Market—was intended to allow exploitation of the same possibility of non-discriminatory discrimination by concentrating the largest tariff reductions on the industrial products in which the United States and Europe jointly dominated the world market. While the "linear" (or "across the board") approach of the Kennedy Round in principle precludes the discrimination possible under the earlier "item-by-item" method, in practice the exceptions lists granted to the bargainers, together with the complicated "tariff disparities" procedure, may leave plenty of room for discrimination against the smaller and less developed countries.

There is, in fact, strong evidence (part of which is presented below) that the principle of non-discrimination as applied in GATT has in practice involved serious discrimination against the less developed countries by the developed countries. There are two main reasons for this, apart from the biases inherent in the negotiating process just discussed.

The first is that although, as GATT was originally envisaged, trade in agricultural products was to be subject to the same rules as trade in industrial products, in fact GATT operates on the rule that domestic agricultural policies override international trading obligations. Agricultural products are relatively far more important in the trade of the less developed countries than in the trade of the developed countries.

Second, the developed industrial countries—primarily Britain and the United States—have used GATT as a medium for the negotiation of special arrangements for trade in cotton textiles, nominally intended to regulate but actually used to restrict the growth of exports of such products by the developing countries. Cotton textiles are the main industry in which the developing countries have established an internationally competitive position, in spite of abnormally high tariff barriers.

Apart entirely from the question of how "non-discrimination" works in practice, there is the more fundamental question of whether non-discrimination is a sensible rule for dealings by one nation with others. Tariffs inherently involve discrimination in favour of resident producers as against foreigners. The presumption is that residents have some special claim on the nation, deriving from their political affiliations to it. If politics make a difference between residents and foreigners, what sense is there in insisting that politics should be allowed to make no difference between foreigners? Politics have in fact made such differences in the past, as evidenced by the Commonwealth preferential system and the association of the overseas territories with the Common Market. These arrangements rested on the special obligations of certain powers to their former colonial territories.

In the present-day world, it can be argued that the developed countries have recognized and assumed responsibility for an obligation to assist the less developed countries to develop, and that this obligation sanctions the establishment of international trading arrangements discriminating in their favour. To put the point another way, it can be argued that the ethical principle embodied in the principle of non-discrimination is the principle that equals should be treated as equals; and that in international economic relations developed countries and less developed countries are not equal.[3]

ARGUMENTS FOR TRADE PREFERENCES

In the documentation and proceedings of the first UNTAD conference, the argument for trade preferences in industrial products for developing countries is presented as "a logical extension of the infant-industry argument." This orientation of the case for preferences is obviously aimed at exploiting the exception allowed by the GATT rules for infant-industry protection. It will not stand serious examination.

Essentially, this argument for preferences is that the markets of the developing countries are too small for the process of "learning by doing" posited by the infant-industry argument to work effectively. Consequently, it is argued, what is required to promote the development of industry in the developing countries is a temporarily protected position in a larger (world) market, such as preferences could give. The proposition that national markets are too small in most underdeveloped countries for protection to produce ultimately efficient production is probably correct. What is involved here, however, is not a logical extension of the infant-industry argument but an empirical emendation of it. For the traditional infant-industry argument contains no stipulation about the size of country required for the argument to be valid. The failure to make such a stipulation is undoubtedly due to the fact that the countries for which the argument was originally advanced—for the United States by Hamilton and for Germany by List—were potentially or actually comparable in size to the contemporary advanced industrial nations. This is not true of the great majority of underdeveloped countries today.

The proposition that most of the underdeveloped countries are too small to benefit from infant-industry protection, however, does not logically lead to the recommendation of preferences in the markets of the developed countries, at least in the generalized form of across-the-board preferences for a fixed period of time advocated at the first UNTAD conference.

In the first place, the traditional infant-industry argument claims that

[3] This point is implicitly accepted in the specially favourable treatment accorded to the protectionist policies of the less developed contracting parties to GATT.

the market process fails to take account of the full social returns from investment in a new industry, and thus sanctions a "social investment" in such industry, this investment to be financed by charging the consumers of the nation a higher price than they would have to pay in the world market. In other words, it recommends a transfer from the consumers to the producers of the nation, a transfer deemed economically beneficial to the nation in the long run. By contrast, the argument for preferences is an argument for a transfer from the consumers (or taxpayers) of the developed countries to the producers of the less developed countries—an inter-national as contrasted with an intra-national income transfer. Logically, the assumption that a market larger than the national market is necessary for the growth of industry into efficient production would lead to the recommendation of production subsidies, not preferences.

Secondly, the infant-industry argument, if fully worked out, implies that protection should be provided on the scale and for the time-period required for the protected industry to establish its competitiveness, if protection is justified at all. This is a very different principle from granting a preferential margin at a common rate and for a common period on the tariffs normally levied on imports of manufactures by developed countries. That principle would involve choosing the extent to which developing-country industries receive protection in developed-country markets not by study of the infant-industry potentialities of the industries in question, but by the levels of protection the developed countries happen to accord to their existing industries. These are not at all closely related to the probable ability of the developing countries to become competitive in these industries.

Moreover, preferences based on existing tariff rates would give the maximum incentives to the establishment in the developing countries of those industries that are subject to the highest protective barriers in the developed countries, and that consequently would face the highest barriers to exports when the temporary protection given by preferences had ended. In this connection, too, it might be noted that, since the grant of protection is generally a reflection of the political influence of the industry receiving it, the basing of preferences on existing tariff rates would entail the maximum threat to the politically most influential industries in the developed countries.

Thirdly, the strength of the argument depends on the reality and strength of the assumed possibilities of infant-industry development. Despite the popularity of the infant-industry (and infant-economy) concept in the conventional wisdom on economic development, no serious effort has been made to test and to prove it, or to show that the inability of less developed countries to export the industrial products they produce is associated with unexploited infant-industry possibilities.

There is, on the contrary, a mounting volume of evidence to the effect that the difficulties of such countries in industrial exporting are attributable to the domestic policies of import-substitution-cum-currency-overvaluation they practise. It is an obvious truism that the economies of large-scale production cannot be realized in a small market. It is less obvious, but probably more important, that modern industry is an intricate network of input-output relationships between firms, and that the effort to force self-sufficiency by protection in a small, industrially-backward economy renders the industry of that economy internationally uncompetitive by raising the costs of manufactured inputs above world levels. This effect of protectionism is not a consequence of the limited size of consumer markets, and could be offset only to a limited extent by trade preferences.

The infant-industry argument for preferences, therefore, carries little conviction. More cogent arguments can, however, be advanced in their support. These arguments necessarily assume: (*a*) that the developed countries have accepted a real obligation to assist the development of the developing countries; (*b*) that, nevertheless, they are for various reasons unwilling to increase their foreign aid programmes substantially; and (*c*) that any massive move towards trade liberalization is not politically feasible in the near future.

In these circumstances, it can be argued that an increase in aid given in the disguised form of trade preferences would be a desirable second-best, and could be sold to the public of the developed countries where a direct increase in aid could not. Moreover, greater exposure of the developing countries to the opportunities and pressures of competition in the world export market is desirable, and if multilateral non-discriminatory liberalization is politically impossible to negotiate, trade preferences might constitute a feasible second-best route to the more desirable objective. Incidentally, these two arguments point to quite different preferential systems, since the former stresses transfers of resources through higher prices, and the latter the beneficent effects of competition in the market.

ARGUMENTS AGAINST TRADE PREFERENCES

Apart from ideological objections deriving from the principle of non-discrimination, discussed above, the arguments against the preference proposal are of two broad sorts: that preferences would do relatively little to promote the exports of the developing countries and that they would involve serious costs. The strength of the second argument obviously depends heavily on the validity of the first (which is discussed in the next section). For, clearly, costs can be considered high or low only in relation to benefits. Nevertheless, the nature of the costs deserves some independent discussion, since the argument from costs so frequently serves as an excuse for doing nothing.

Two kinds of cost have been advanced in argument against preferences: the administrative costs of operating a preferential system, and what may be called the "moral risks" of introducing the preferential principle.

The administrative costs would depend on the type of preferential system adopted, and would clearly increase with the degree to which preferences discriminated among developing countries and the extent to which quotas were used to control trade. The addition to administrative costs entailed by preferences, however, may easily be exaggerated, given the overhead cost inherent in any customs system and the complexity of present tariff legislation. In this connection, it is worth recalling that in 1958 an OEEC expert group found that it would be administratively feasible to associate the other European countries with the Common Market in a European Free Trade Area, in spite of the alleged insuperability of the "trade-deflection" problem.

The alleged moral risks are that preferences would create a strong vested interest against further multilateral trade liberalization, and that a preferential scheme would have to be approved by the U.S. Congress, which might take the opportunity to indulge in an orgy of domestic protectionism, favouritism towards particular developing countries, and retaliation against particular developed countries. The vested-interest argument is not very persuasive, since the developing countries having the interest would not be directly represented in the policy-making of the developed countries giving the preferences; and once the preferences were established the economic foolishness of discriminating against efficient producers in developed countries in favour of inefficient producers in developing countries might generate public pressure for lower tariffs all round. Further, the establishment of preferences would probably have to be accompanied by the development of adjustment assistance techniques for the domestic producers adversely affected by the new competition, and so pave the way for a bolder assault on tariff barriers.

The fear of what the U.S. Congress might do if offered the chance to jettison the principle of non-discrimination is a powerful force in American official thinking on commercial policy questions. The dangers can be amply illustrated by reference to the favouritism and the lobbying activity that accompany the fixing of the U.S. sugar import quotas. It is, however, both insulting and defeatist to regard the Congress merely as an irresponsible collection of narrow self-seeking politicians who cannot be trusted to legislate in the public interest. Congress in the past has been inspired to heights of true statesmanship—and not always in reluctant submission to the *force majeure* of able Presidential leadership—and it has shown itself capable of great generosity toward the less developed countries. There is no real justification for assuming that it could not be induced to accept a preferential system that would genuinely help the less developed countries.

TRADE PREFERENCES AND DEVELOPMENT

The crucial question is how far trade preferences could serve to promote economic development, or, more concretely and manageably, to promote the industrial exports of the less developed countries. The most careful statement available of the view that preferences would do relatively little in this respect has been provided by Professor Gardner Patterson, in the article in this *Review* referred to earlier.

Starting from the estimate that the average *ad valorem* tariff rate on manufactured goods in the advanced industrial countries is now about 15 per cent, Patterson assumes that the Kennedy Round of negotiations will be successful eventually in reducing such tariffs by about 35 per cent, to an average of 10 per cent. He then remarks that the advanced countries would be reluctant to give preferences resulting in "zero duties," and assumes a 50 per cent preference, yielding a preference margin of 5 per cent. Finally, he concludes that the industries in which a preference margin of 5-7 per cent would enable less developed countries to take markets away from domestic and developed-country competitors, excluding those cases where a non-discriminatory tariff reduction would do as well, constitute a very short list indeed.

Even on its own terms, this argument leaves something to be desired as an assessment of the potentialities of preferences. First, as intervening events have shown, it is premature to take credit for a successful conclusion of the Kennedy round. Second, it is invalid to use the assumption that only limited preferences will be given, to prove that preferences would have little economic effect. And third, it is not legitimate to exclude commodities for which non-discriminatory tariff reductions would do as well, since there is no reason to expect that such reductions will, in fact, take place.

EFFECTIVE TARIFF RATES

The fundamental objections to this analysis, however, relate to the use of nominal tariff rates to assess the barriers to trade inherent in existing tariff schedules. Tariff averages conceal the fact that tariff rates tend to be significantly higher than average on the consumer goods in which the developing countries have an actual or potential exporting capacity. Of much greater importance, the protective effects of tariff schedules on domestic production cannot be evaluated by reference to the duty rate on commodities. They must be measured by the effective rates of protection of the value added in the production processes that turn out the goods.

Imported goods are used in a modern industrial economy both as raw materials for domestic production (inputs) and as substitutes for home-produced goods. Tariffs on imported substitutes provide protection to domestic producers, but tariffs on imported inputs constitute a tax on domestic producers. To arrive at the net protective effect, it is necessary to calculate the net subsidy (or possibly tax) on value added in an industry provided by the entire tariff schedule. When this is done, it turns out that effective protection rates on manufactures are typically $1\frac{1}{2}$ times to twice as high as the nominal tariff rates, and that they rise progressively with the stage of production or degree of fabrication of the product.[4]

This fundamental point is illustrated by . . . a recent empirical study

[4] A hypothetical example may help to show how this conclusion is reached. Suppose a commodity has a world price of $1.00, of which $0.60 represents raw materials and $0.40 the value added by foreign producers. Assume imports of the commodity are subject to a tariff of 15 per cent, while domestic producers have to pay a tariff of 5 per cent on their raw materials. The domestic producer can thus incur a maximum expenditure of $1.15 to produce the commodity. How much more can he spend on value added than the foreigner? This is the effective rate of protection.

	Foreign Product $	*Domestic Product* $
Domestic market price	1.15	1.15
Price to producer	1.00	1.15
Cost of materials	0.60	0.63
Price chargeable for value added	0.40	0.52

The excess of domestic over foreign value added is $0.12, which, as a percentage of foreign value added, is 30 per cent. This is the *effective protection rate,* equal to the difference between the gross subsidy on value added provided by the tariff on the final product $\left(\frac{.15}{.40} = 37\frac{1}{2} \text{ per cent}\right)$ and the *implicit tax on value added* as a result of the tariff on raw materials $\left(\frac{.03}{.40} = 7\frac{1}{2} \text{ per cent}\right)$.

by Professor Bela Balassa. This demonstrates fully that the order of magnitude of the barriers that less developed countries have to face in competing with producers in developed countries is not the 15 per cent average cited by Patterson, but rather something in the neighbourhood of 25 to 50 per cent, and in particular cases even higher. It is in this context that the stimulus to industrial exports that might be provided by preferences needs to be evaluated.

As is well known, preferences have two sorts of effect on trade. They create trade by enabling the preference-receiving producers to compete more effectively with domestic producers, and they divert trade from non-preferred to preferred suppliers. In the context of the effective protection concept, the trade-creating incentive might be substantially greater than the calculated effective protection rates would suggest. For the preference might reduce the subsidy to domestic production given by the tariff on the finished good, without reducing the taxation of domestic production implicit in the tariffs levied on other goods used as inputs in the production process.

. . . With respect to trade diversion, the calculated effective protection rates are irrelevant, since foreign producers do not pay domestic tariffs on their raw materials. Here the relevant consideration indicated by the effective protection concept is that the incentive to trade diversion is measured not by the extent to which it allows the price of the preferred producer's product to be higher than his rival's, but by the extent to which it allows him to charge more for the value added to those inputs that are equally available in the world market to all competitors. Since value added typically runs somewhat under one half of sales value, one might guess that the premium on value added given by a preference would be roughly about twice the margin of preference on the commodity produced.

. . . Moreover, since, in the long run, capital, like the raw materials used in production, is freely mobile between countries, preferences should probably be conceived essentially as paying a premium for the use of the preference-receiving nation's labour over the labour of its competitors. On this basis, a small margin of preference on the finished product might amount to a very high premium indeed on labour cost. Concretely, small margins of preference might have a powerful effect in inducing enterprises domiciled in advanced countries to establish production facilities in developing countries in order to circumvent the tariffs levied on their direct exports to other developed countries.

Analysis on effective protection lines, therefore, indicates that, within existing tariff structures, trade preferences for developing countries, even if not at the 100 per cent level, might provide powerful incentives for the expansion of their industrial exports. Would the developing countries, however, be able to respond effectively to such export opportunities? As already mentioned, their price and cost levels are often well above world market levels, and frequently the excess is substantially greater than the tariff-created excess of domestic over world market prices in the developed countries. In such cases, even 100 per cent preferences could not offset the competitive disadvantage. It would appear that preferences would be of no avail unless they were accompanied by drastic reform of the currency-overvaluation and protectionist import-substitution policies that make these countries unable to compete in world markets.

TRADE PREFERENCES AND TRADE LIBERALIZATION

Preferential trading arrangements may be designed for either of two contrasting purposes: to extend the area of protection, or to extend the area of free competition. The spirit of the demand for trade preferences voiced at the first UNTAD conference was definitely protectionist, and so, in the main, has been the response of those in the developed countries who favour the proposal. Preferential arrangements for less developed countries could be devised, however, that would be trade-liberalizing in spirit. Such arrangements would seek to maximize trade creation and to minimize trade diversion. This would require, in broad terms, concentrating the preferences on products in which the developed countries have a visible comparative disadvantage and the less developed countries an established or potential comparative advantage: broadly speaking, on products demanding only unskilled or semi-skilled labour and relatively little capital, and which employ a relatively simply technology. The objective would be a "new international division of labour," to be achieved by a planned transfer of such industries from the developed countries to the less developed countries.

The process would be politically unpopular on both sides. The developed countries would have to devise policies for the planned contraction or extermination of established protected industries. The less developed countries would have to give up their aspirations for industrial self-sufficiency. But it would contribute both to increased efficiency in the utilization of the world's human and material resources, and to the economic development of the less developed world. There would be no need to rely on the infant-industry argument; and the preferences could be installed as a permanent feature of world trading relationships (subject to reduction by future non-discriminatory trade liberalization), thus avoiding the complexities of administering temporary preferences.

COMMODITY AGREEMENTS: BONANZA OR ILLUSION?

John A. Pincus

A major plank in the UNCTAD platform is the establishment of commodity agreements to raise and stabilize LDC earnings from their traditional exports. This article, by the editor, examines the possibilities and limitations of such agreements.

Kwame Nkrumah loiters in Guinea, a solitary redeemer, savoring memories of former potency and dreaming of power as yet untasted. A protesting Sukarno slides inexorably down a pole greased by his cabinet ministers. Middle Eastern sheiks command without deftness a power that their fathers, in mud-walled isolation, could never aspire to, even in the most paranoid of reveries.

These vagaries, which help to shape the world's political destinies, all reflect in part the fluctuations of world markets for commodities—the foodstuffs and raw materials that enter world trade. Nkrumah suffered politically from the consequences of falling prices for cocoa; Sukarno from declining rubber prices and reductions in export volume for tin and rubber; while the Middle East rides a petroleum boom.

Each of these examples deals with underdeveloped countries. This is no accident, because only in the poor countries of the world is commodity production—farming, forestry, and mining—the principal source of income. Many of the rich nations, such as the United States, Canada, Australia, and the Scandinavian countries, are major producers and exporters of commodities. In fact, the rich countries export half of the world's primary commodities, but only a small part of their population is employed in commodity production, and only a small part of government revenues stem from commodity taxes. Even Australia, Canada, and New

John A. Pincus, "Commodity Agreements: Bonanza or Illusion?" *Columbia Journal of World Business* 2, No. 1 (January, 1967), 41-50. Reprinted by permission of the publishers.

Zealand, which export mostly commodities, today produce much more manufactured goods than commodities.

No wonder therefore that the pressure for world commodity controls comes largely from poor countries allegedly seeking to stabilize, but really to increase, their export earnings. Commodity export earnings account for a large part of their total production, with most of the people living and working as farmers. Exports of commodities (or in some cases capital inflows) are the prime source for financing the capital imports that they need now in order to become rich later. Furthermore, when commodity exports are booming, export taxes and import duties offer the governments a ready source of revenue to finance the ambitions of a Sukarno or a Nkrumah, as well as the less flamboyant goals of an Eduardo Frei in Chile, or a Kenneth Kaunda in Zambia.

PLEA FOR INTERNATIONAL RESCUE

Most poor countries seek rapid economic growth, which inevitably generates inflationary pressures and the demand for imports. Increases in commodity export earnings are therefore seen as a key to development without excessive inflation. Large-scale export of manufactured products still seems remote, and accounts now for only one-tenth of underdeveloped countries' exports. Finally, the governments of most poor countries take it as an article of faith that the terms of trade of commodity exporting countries are in a long-term decline that can only be overcome by conscious international action. Otherwise, in their view, as expressed in the resolutions of the United Nations Conference on Trade And Development (UNCTAD), the normal operation of world trade will tend to make the rich nations richer and the poor nations poorer.

This pressure for higher commodity prices has generally been resisted by the industrial importing countries, despite their own widespread use of farm price supports as a means of transferring income to farmers. Their standard arguments against price control through international commodity agreements are:

(1) They interfere with normal operation of markets, and tend to build up surplus production in response to higher prices; pressure of these supplies leads to breakdown of agreements, or at least to erosion of their effects on price.

(2) Because commodity agreements are usually based on export quota systems, they tend to freeze historical production patterns, to the disadvantage of efficient producers.

(3) They require a complex apparatus for control of exports and supply, which is further complicated by the existence of different grades of each commodity, each of which has a submarket of its own with fluctuating prices.

(4) Price and output controls, as established in commodity agreements, are an inefficient way to redistribute world income, as compared to direct subsidy, because price controls lead to less efficient production and lesser satisfaction of consumer preference than subsidies do.

(5) The income-redistributing effects of higher commodity prices may mean in effect that low-income consumers in industrial countries are forced to pay for improvements in the living standards of high-income producers in the underdeveloped countries.

The controversy between governments of rich and poor countries has been thoroughly confused because they are simultaneously discussing several different issues without necessarily recognizing it.

First of all, much of the discussion of commodity agreements stresses price stability as an objective at least coequal with higher prices. Thus the UNCTAD resolution on the subject calls for: "suitable international arrangements . . . designed to *increase and stabilize* primary commodity export earnings, particularly of developing countries, at equitable and remunerative prices. . . ."

In fact, stabilizing earnings as such (i.e., smoothing out periodic fluctuations around a trend) is a trivial goal in poor countries' eyes. It has been much stressed, however, for two reasons: (1) year-to-year commodity price fluctuations are dramatic, and the advantages of greater stability, in terms of central economic planning and private investment, seem both obvious and ideologically innocuous; and (2) the stabilization goal offers an acceptable argument for introducing international commodity agreements, which can then be used to raise prices to "remunerative" levels.

STABILIZATION SMOKESCREEN

Statistical evidence indicates that short-term fluctuations in export earnings do not slow down economic development, as compared to steady annual receipts. Though this statement is the reverse of what is usually said by spokesmen of poor countries, the proof-of-the-pudding principle casts substantial doubt on their contentions. If a country wants to stabilize annual export revenues, it has only to set money aside in good years, and spend it in bad ones. Yet very few countries do this.[1] The obvious answer is that poor countries lack the reserves to finance such stabilization in light of their aspirations for development. While this proposition may be perfectly valid, those who offer it frequently fail to recognize that it amounts to a demand for more foreign exchange in the guise of stabilization goals. Alasdair MacBean's exhaustive study of this subject[2] indicates that there has been no correlation in recent decades between income growth in poor countries and export fluctuations. Indeed, MacBean's conclusion, based on extensive analysis, is that short-run fluctuations in national income bear very little relation to fluctuations in export earnings. To the extent that short-term balance-of-payments problems arise entirely as a result of short-term fluctuations around an earnings trend, IMF credits, bilateral loans, and suppliers' credits are readily available; poor countries appear to feel no urgent need for additional safeguards aimed solely at the objective of stabilizing year-to-year earnings. What poor countries do want is higher prices (or at least no decline in prices) for commodities; "stabilization" objectives are primarily a tactic toward that goal.

A second source of confusion is between fact and theory about underdeveloped countries' terms of trade (export prices divided by import prices). According to theories developed by the Argentinian economist, Raúl Prebisch, who now serves as Secretary-General of UNCTAD, there are inexorable forces at work tending to reduce the prices of commodities relative to manufactured products. This tends to hurt poor countries, which export mostly commodities, and to benefit rich countries, which import commodities and export manufactured products. In support of this view, Prebisch has argued that underdeveloped countries' terms of trade have in fact fallen since the latter part of the 19th century. He has been challenged by a number of economists, both as to theory and fact, but unfortunately the distinctions between logic and observation have not always been maintained. The theoretical objections point to a number of inconsistencies in his rather complex argument. The empirical ones question the data he has cited and argue that conclusions as to the long-term course of terms of trade depend on the choice of base period.

[1] The commodity marketing boards in West African countries were designed to operate in such a manner, and during the era of high commodity prices following the Korean War actually amassed considerable reserves. The combination of declining prices and pressures to spend reserves, stimulated by postindependence developmental goals, has largely succeeded in eliminating the income-stabilizing functions of the marketing boards.

[2] Alasdair MacBean, *Export Instability and Economic Development* (Cambridge: Harvard University Press, 1967).

PRIMARY PRODUCER CAN BOUNCE BACK

No final conclusions about either fact or theory seem to be possible as yet. In recent years world demand for most major commodities other than petroleum has increased slowly compared to demand for goods and services in general, while commodity supplies have increased rather rapidly, thanks to the stimulus of high prices in the 1950's, the growth of synthetic output (particularly fiber and rubber) and protectionist policies in the rich countries. It may however be doubted whether world commodity prices will long continue sluggish or declining if world population continues to increase at current rates.

A third source of confusion lies in the debate about what commodity agreements can accomplish. The poor countries, supported at UNCTAD by the government of France, sometimes appear to claim that higher commodity prices, secured by international agreement, are a source of instant prosperity. Most rich countries seem to argue that commodity agreements could not be effective in raising prices above market levels, but only in stabilizing prices over a cycle. This contention in its extreme form is obviously wrong, as witness the high prices paid to farmers in countries where agriculture is protected, or the high prices received for crude petroleum by low-cost exporters in the Middle East and Venezuela. The confusion lies both in the effort of rich countries to prove that because the policy is undesirable, or leads to administrative complications, it is therefore impossible; and in the effort of poor countries to show that because high commodity prices have often been beneficial in the past, they can therefore be legislated as a development panacea for the future.

This last dispute of course reflects the fact that each side assumes away the obstacles to its case and, thereby, simply sidesteps the central issues: What are the effects of commodity agreements on price? Who pays and who benefits from the higher prices? What commodities could be subject to effective international action in the interests of underdeveloped countries? Could the objectives of commodity agreements be met more easily by other devices that are both feasible technically *and* likely to be adopted?

THE TROUBLE WITH SUBSIDIES

It is clear that rich countries can pay poor countries any "price" they want for commodity exports. There is no logical, constitutional, or economic barrier to doubling or tripling the revenues that underdeveloped countries receive for commodity exports. This has nothing to do with whether demand is elastic (revenues declining in response to price rises) or inelastic (revenues rising in response to higher prices). If, for example, the governments of industrial countries want to pay some amount into an economic development fund for each pound of coffee they import, that sum can be as large as the generosity of governments allows. It is simply a subsidy to coffee-growing countries, and there is no limit to the amount of a subsidy.

But subsidies are not a popular technique for supporting farmers' incomes. The technique of operating through market prices via supply control is universally preferred by farmers and governments, because the consequent income transfer takes on the status of an impersonal market transaction rather than a gift, and does not enter as an item in the government budget. Furthermore, there is no particular reason to tie direct subsidy into commodity production. If rich countries want to subsidize poor ones, they can do it by foreign aid appropriations rather than subsidies to commodity exporters.

LONG LIST, BUT MANY HITCHES

Therefore the income-increasing objectives of international commodity agreements are expected to operate through supply restriction. These techniques can normally succeed in raising producers' incomes only if demand for their output is inelastic.[3] Demand for a number of the major commodities in world trade is quite inelastic. The principal traded commodities are, in order of trade value: petroleum, meat, wheat, fats and vegetable oils, cotton, coffee, copper, wool, sugar, rubber, dairy products, tobacco, rice, corn, tea, cocoa, tin, jute, zinc, lead, bananas, and citrus fruit. The combined annual value of trade in these products is about $35 billion.

There are, however, a few hitches that would cause a number of these products to be dropped from any list of candidates for price-fixing agreements aimed at benefiting underdeveloped countries. Petroleum, accounting for nearly $10 billion of exports, is already subject to international price fixing by private agreements between oil companies and governments of the major petroleum-exporting countries. Meat, wheat, wool, dairy products and corn, amounting to an additional $5 billion, are primarily exported by rich countries, so that price-fixing schemes would

[3] Exporting governments can profit from higher prices even under elastic demand, if the labor and capital released from commodity production can be effectively used in other economic activities. But the mobility of labor and capital in poor countries is often quite limited.

hurt poor countries more as consumers than it would benefit them as exporters. Of the remaining sixteen products, six (oils and fats, citrus fruits, tobacco, copper, lead and zinc) are exported in substantial quantities by both rich and poor countries, so that the United States, Canada, Australia, Spain, and South Africa would be major beneficiaries of price-fixing schemes. This difficulty is not necessarily crippling, because these countries could presumably agree to pay their "profits" into a fund for the benefit of developing countries. However, these products present other problems for regulation. Nonferrous metals substitute for each other (and for plastics in some uses), so that the price of each would have to be regulated in light of all others. Vegetable and animal fats and oils also substitute for each other (and for synthetic detergents), so that the problems created by control efforts would be even more complex than for metals. Citrus fruits are close substitutes for other fruits in the consumer budget. Finally, since each of these products, or a close substitute, is produced in a number of the major importing countries, a rise in the world price might lead to substitution of home production for imports, unless importers agreed to maintain home production at preexisting levels.

This leaves 10 major traded commodities for initial consideration under price-fixing schemes aimed at benefiting underdeveloped areas: cotton, coffee, sugar, rubber, rice, tea, cocoa, tin, jute, and bananas. All of these products are primarily exported by poor countries.

Jute and rubber are ruled out from the start, unless other textile fibers and synthetic rubber prices are also controlled. General control of world fiber prices seems out of the question, and while joint control of natural and synthetic rubber prices is theoretically possible, the countries that produce synthetic rubber show no interest in such a program.

AND THEN THERE WERE SIX

Cotton and rice are special cases in that the United States is a major exporter. Even if the United States renounced its potential profits under price-fixing schemes, other difficulties would arise. Raising cotton prices again implies control of other fiber prices, both natural and synthetic. The problem with rice is that underdeveloped countries are the principal importers, so that raising the price simply helps producers in some underdeveloped countries at the expense of consumers in poor countries. Furthermore, such a price rise would simply stimulate production in the importing countries.

The 10 products therefore reduce to six. The following table shows the average value of trade in each for the years 1959-61.

Product	Value of Exports (millions of $)
Coffee	1,878
Tea	616
Cocoa	521
Sugar	1,498
Tin	392
Bananas	334
Total	5,239

Two of these products, coffee and tin, are now organized under international commodity agreements. Tea was marketed under a commodity agreement from 1933 to 1939, as was sugar intermittently from 1931 to 1961. Negotiations for an international cocoa agreement have been proceeding without success since 1958. Bananas, produced exclusively in the tropics, are probably ruled out because of competition with other fruits, both imported and domestic.

MORE FROM THE LAGGARDS

I have indicated elsewhere[4] that establishment of effective price-fixing agreements for these products, excluding tin, might have succeeded in raising underdeveloped countries' export earnings by $450-$900 million in 1961. The United States would currently pay about 35 per cent to 40 per cent of this total, and the other major industrial nations the following per cent shares: United Kingdom, 11-12; France, 7-8; Japan, 6-9; Germany 8-10. These percentages are based on estimates of each country's elasticity of demand for each of these products at monopoly price levels.

If these monopoly prices were in effect, the upshot would be to increase the relative share of western foreign aid now paid by some of the laggard donors—U.K., Japan, and Germany—and decrease the shares of the major donors, United States and France. United States and France now provide respectively about 60 per cent and 17 per cent of western foreign aid. If their aid through commodity pricing were respectively 35-40 per cent and 7-8 per cent of total western costs under a system of commodity agreements, then their relative share of total official aid would be reduced.

But the most important point to note from these figures is not their effects on the distribution of foreign-aid costs, but their total amount: $450-$900 million in 1961, rising to more than $1 billion by 1970, and

[4] John Pincus, *Trade, Aid, and Development* (New York: McGraw-Hill Book Company, 1967).

nearly $2 billion by 1975. This compares with 1965 capital flows from rich to poor countries of about $9 billion, and poor countries' total merchandise exports of $36 billion. By 1970, capital flows may not have changed substantially from 1961 levels, while export values will have risen to about $45 billion if current trends are followed.

The effects of monopoly pricing on export earnings would therefore be modest, but far from insignificant. This after all is what we would expect. The price of coffee (and the earnings of coffee exporters) has risen about 20 per cent since the International Coffee Agreement was negotiated in 1962. Meanwhile, the world price of sugar has fallen to record low levels since the break-up of the Sugar Agreement in 1961, with disastrous effects on those exporters who depend heavily on world market sales. There is obviously a relation between prices of these products and exporters' foreign exchange earnings.

FIVE INGREDIENTS

But signing agreements is no guarantee of high prices, high export earnings, or favorable effects on economic development. For the agreements to work effectively as agents of development goals, several conditions are required, in addition to inelastic long-run demand:

(1) Effective provisions for control over supply (not only export control, because when supply builds up, the pressures for breakup of the agreement become strong);

(2) Effective capacity on the part of existing governments to channel the increased earnings into economic development, rather than into higher profits for plantation owners;

(3) Less generally recognized, a market organization in which one or two producing countries dominate world supply, so that they are willing to practice restraint in the face of the inevitable supply control violations by smaller producers;

(4) A large number of producing countries, in order to assure a fairly wide distribution of gains from higher prices;

(5) Agreement to limit domestic production in those importing countries that can or do produce the commodity.

Let us take a look at existing and proposed commodity agreements in light of these criteria. First of all, it should be noted that the impetus behind most of them was the desire to stem price erosion rather than to achieve some maximum long-run level of earnings for producers. However, in terms of development goals, the issues listed above are nonetheless predominant.

TEA, WITH SUGAR

The Tea Agreement (1933-1939) clearly succeeded in stabilizing world prices during the depression, but its impact on development may be doubted. Most of India's and Ceylon's tea gardens were under British control, and the benefits of earnings' stabilization largely accrued to the plantation owners. Furthermore, with tea production then largely concentrated in four Asian countries, the benefits were also concentrated geographically. These very limitations made it relatively easy to control tea supplies. With a small number of large producers and a very inelastic demand for the product, each could see his advantage in cooperating in export control. Furthermore, tea can be "stored" on the bush, so that control can be exercised up to a point by picking more or fewer leaves at any time.

The Sugar Agreement (1931-1961) was a completely different matter. In the first place, the agreement covered only the so-called "free market," accounting for perhaps two-fifths of world trade. The rest of the world's imports are controlled by national legislation, notably British, American, and French import systems, under which each country imports from preferred suppliers at a premium price. The essence of the Sugar Agreement, as operated from 1954 to 1961, was a bargain by which Cuba, as the dominant free market supplier, agreed to manage its supplies and stocks, in exchange for its large quota in the high-priced U.S. market. The objective was to maintain world prices between 3.25 and 4.25 cents per pound, through a system of export quotas. The system worked moderately well until 1960, when the United States first reduced and then abolished the Cuban quota. The agreement has not been renewed since 1961, when Cuba insisted on and was refused a large increase in its basic quota. It presumably will not be renewed until the underlying political issues are overcome.

Any effort to maintain very high prices for sugar (more than 5 or 6 cents a pound in the long run) is probably self-defeating, even though world demand for sugar is increasing steadily. Unlike tea, sugar can be produced almost anywhere, even if at high cost. Therefore if prices rise, and are expected to remain high under a system of export control, production in importing countries would tend to rise sharply. This puts sharp limits on the price objectives that exporting countries could aspire to. In these circumstances, it is arguable that developing countries would gain more from free trade in sugar than from price manipulation. However, the tendency seems to be for more rather than less agricultural protectionism in importing countries, so that a sugar agreement still retains considerably more luster in exporters' eyes than the unlikely alternative of free trade.

TIN STAYS BUOYANT

The Tin Agreement (1954 to date) operates under some of the same conditions as the earlier Tea Agreement. There are only five major signatory exporters (Malaya, Indonesia, Thailand, China, Bolivia), dominated by Malaya; there are a relatively small number of producing units. Tin, like tea, can be "stored" easily, either by mining less, or by stockpiling. The agreement provided for a buffer stock, in addition to export quotas, which helped to manage supply. The buffer stock manager bought tin when prices fell below a floor level and sold it when they rose above a given ceiling. After considerable price fluctuations in the 1950's, the world price of tin began to rise in 1960. By 1961, the buffer stock was sold out of tin, all export quotas were off, and world prices since have been consistently far above the pre-1961 levels. The agreement remains in effect inoperative today, because of continued strong demand. Both floor and ceiling prices were raised when the agreement was last renewed (1965). The presumption is that tin prices will therefore remain well above the levels that led to the original agreement.

As in the case of tea, it may be questioned whether international action in the world tin market is a significant force in promoting economic development. Concentration of production is great, and although Bolivian, Indonesian, and Chinese governments, with their nationalized tin industries, clearly benefit from the rise in price, Bolivia is the only one that is heavily dependent on tin exports as a source of income.

COFFEE IS SUCCESSFUL; OR IS IT?

The International Coffee Agreement, negotiated in 1962, has clearly succeeded in maintaining export earnings of coffee producers above equilibrium levels by a system of export quotas. As might be expected, its very success threatens the stability of the agreement. By providing high and stable prices for coffee, it tempts producers to evade export controls. It therefore places a great burden of self-restraint on the major producers, Brazil and Colombia, who face erosion of their market shares at the hands of Central American and African producers. These smaller producers are unwilling to establish close control over exports and production. Even though importing members are theoretically unable to take extra-quota imports from exporting members, there seems to be a good deal of evasion in the form of transshipments through non-member countries or so-called "new markets" not subject to the quota provisions.

In terms of many of the criteria discussed—demand elasticity, substitution, widespread benefits—coffee is an appropriate product for price-fixing arrangements. But the willingness and ability of the smaller producers to control supply still remains an open question, and it may be doubted that Brazil will consent to continual reduction of her share of the world coffee market by what are in effect extra-legal methods of quota evasion on the part of small producers. Recent modifications of the Coffee Agreement are designed in part to solve this problem.

CHANGING THE RULES

The agreement is administered by a Coffee Council, composed of representatives of importing and exporting countries. The council regularly receives pleas for export increases from members who are unable or unwilling to control production and exports. The agreement assigns fixed percentages of the export market to each exporter so that selective quota changes are theoretically forbidden. In practice, however, when the alternative is collapse of the agreement, the council has devised ways of changing the rules. The most recent set of rule changes, adopted in September, 1966, is worth reviewing in detail as the first consistent effort to deal with the obstacles to price-fixing objectives and economic development goals.

First, the council explicitly recognized that the world coffee market is composed of submarkets for the four main types of coffee: Brazilian arabica, Colombian and Central American arabica, and African robusta. In the future, export quotas will vary by coffee type. This will presumably allow the major robusta producers (Ivory Coast, Cameroons, Angola) to increase their exports faster than other growers, reflecting the steady growth of demand for the lower-priced robusta in instant coffee preparations. It also offers an additional advantage: robusta producers generally complain that their quotas are too small under the existing agreement, and these producers are also often the least able to control production and exports.

A second element of the revised agreement combines temporary quota increases of varying percentages (zero for Brazil and Colombia and up to 10 per cent for some African producers) with use of the proceeds to promote production control. Each country receiving a quota increase agrees to put into a special fund either 20 per cent of the increased sales proceeds, or an amount of coffee equal to the amount of the quota increase. Each country will use the fund, under rules established by the Coffee Council, to promote agricultural diversification. This provision is presumably aimed both at promoting the economic development of the exporting countries and at meeting the objections of Brazil and Colombia to the perpetual growth of uncontrolled supply in other countries.

The third element proposed in 1966 (but not yet adopted) was a tax of one dollar on each bag of coffee exported under the agreement, to be paid by the exporting country. This would produce a revenue of about $45 million during the current marketing year. The proceeds would be used to finance programs of agricultural diversification, under control of the Coffee Council.

Finally, the council took steps to limit evasion of export quotas. Importing members agreed to limit their imports from nonmembers. Beginning in 1967, exporting members cannot ship coffee unless the export documents bear a stamp obtained from the Coffee Council. These devices can also be viewed as efforts to satisfy Brazilian demands for more effective control over world supply.

OUTLOOK ON COCOA

Among the major products discussed here, only cocoa and bananas have not yet been subject to international commodity controls. Cocoa qualifies on many of the same grounds as coffee, but is difficult to store in the tropics, and faces a greater threat of competition, either from vegetable oils (used in place of cocoa butter) or from other confectioneries. Efforts at agreement failed in both 1963 and 1966, because of disagreements between producers and consumers as to the price at which export quotas would become operative. More recently, it has been suggested that a cocoa agreement include provision for a buffer stock, along the lines of the tin agreement, in order to maintain price within agreed limits. A cocoa agreement would provide a number of the prerequisites: one or two major exporters (Ghana, Nigeria), large numbers of producers, inelastic demand, good possibility of devoting excess profits to development goals. It is less certain that the African countries can effectively control supplies. This is probably one major reason for their insistence on an international buffer stock. Unfortunately, the producing countries seem reluctant to recognize that buffer stocks exist not only to buy, but also to sell, so that the buffer stock cannot be relied on as a permanent siphon for excess production. There seems to be little doubt that a cocoa agreement, in some form, will be negotiated by 1968. But it is not clear whether it will be acceptable to all parliaments, notably the United States Congress.

IS IT ALL WORTH THE EFFORT?

This review of the major products suitable for conscious efforts at price fixing shows that the possibilities are limited, the complexities of production control great, and the technique essentially inefficient as compared to direct aid. Furthermore, as noted above, the export quota system offers little incentive to efficient new producers, because it freezes an historical production pattern, without much regard for changing cost and demand patterns (although it is theoretically possible to adjust export quotas selectively, no exporter wants his share reduced).

Coffee and cocoa are widely produced by individual farmers, so the allegation that high prices benefit only the plantation owner is clearly untrue for these crops. For sugar and tea, the charge may be closer to the mark, although there are many small producers and export taxes can be used to siphon off excess profits, unless the government is dominated by producer interest. Tin is a rather special case where demand has long been buoyant; half the world's output stems from nationalized industries (Bolivia, Indonesia, China, Russia) and most of the rest from Malaya. There seems no particular reason to believe that for these five products the distribution of gains from higher commodity earnings need be more inequitable than those stemming from other forms of aid (except food aid, which presumably benefits low-income groups most).

Recent developments in the Coffee Agreement indicate that commodity agreements may be a more flexible device for promoting economic adjustment than was previously supposed. It is obviously too early to judge the success of these measures in their dual objectives of controlling coffee supply and promoting the agricultural development of exporting countries. The most significant element is clearly the diversification fund. In embryo at least, it foreshadows a principle of international control of the proceeds of monopoly pricing in the interest of economic development. In that respect, the Coffee Agreement becomes, in part, an aspect of international economic assistance under the joint policy control of rich and poor countries. This novel organizational device may, if successful, offer broad possibilities for application to other commodities and, for that matter, for other forms of economic aid.

However, this qualified support for a limited number of commodity agreements is, from another viewpoint, an admission of their weakness as answers to the world's commodity problems. Such agreements are only one element in a general policy to improve the trade position of commodity-exporting countries. The other elements include:

(1) Major efforts to increase the productivity of industries facing competition from synthetic substitutes or competing production in importing countries (rubber, fibers, sugar, rice, oilseeds).

(2) Reduction of protectionism in importing countries (petroleum, sugar, tobacco, nonferrous metals, fruits, meat, etc.); this is probably the largest potential source of increased exports for poor countries. Free trade in sugar alone might increase underdeveloped countries' exports earnings by nearly one billion dollars, at least as much as the amounts forthcoming from price-fixing agreements for coffee, cocoa, sugar, tea and tin combined.

(3) A system of international compensation for countries whose export earnings lag over a period of several years because of market factors beyond their policy control (e.g., Brazil from 1959 to 1963); this would be in addition to existing IMF loan facilities for countries facing short-term balance-of-payments problems that have arisen from commodity price fluctuations.

The excessive emphasis that the poor countries have placed on high prices reflects in part ignorance of the limitations of this technique; in part, the related belief that economic justice requires a fair price for exports; and, perhaps most important, pessimism about the likelihood of trade liberalization by the rich countries. But their confidence in price-fixing seems misplaced; the experience of the past five years makes it increasingly clear that no panacea will emerge. Each of the four elements —price objectives, higher productivity, trade liberalization, and balance-of-payments compensation—should play a part in a long-run adjustment effort for the nearly two billion people whose livelihoods now depend on commodity production. As long as the economic welfare of most people depends on markets for food and raw materials, the commodity problem will remain in the center stage of the world's political economy.

THE HOROWITZ PROPOSAL

David Horowitz

Mr. David Horowitz, Governor of the Bank of Israel, has been an effective spokesman for more generous aid policies toward less developed countries. At the 1964 UNCTAD Conference, he proposed a system of international borrowing in the capital markets of rich countries, with the proceeds to be relent at subsidized interest rates to the LDCs. His proposal was included in the Final Act of UNCTAD, and the following excerpt is taken from his statement to the Conference.

How is it that the United States could finance the reconstruction of Europe by the most generous and formidable Marshall Plan pioneering in the field of economic assistance within a few years after an exhausting war and when it had to supply the pent-up demand in its own country? This was done by the United States alone, while now the whole developed world is faced with the challenge of development of the underprivileged part of humanity, when the resources on both sides of the Ocean are incomparably larger.

How is it that several major countries could spend so many billions for space exploration, and succeed so splendidly and the problem of development should remain unsolved?

The gap is widening and it is our duty to subject the record of our failure to a remorseless scrutiny. There are no insuperable obstacles independent of our will and our effort on the road to a better life for the whole world. It is not the first time that fallacies in thinking and prejudices, that financial ultra-orthodoxy is defeating a desirable and great end. Now we know that the Irish Famine could have been relieved without much difficulty were it not for the fallacies of economic thinking, of a mistaken belief in iron laws which could not be bent. Now we know

David Horowitz, "The Horowitz Proposal," statement of the delegate of Israel to the United Nations Conference on Trade and Development, Geneva, Switzerland, 1964.

that the great crises of the 20's and 30's in Europe and America and of the whole developed world could have been averted by proper measures. The proof of that certainty is that such crises have never been repeated since the Second World War. We should beware of becoming again the prisoners of our own prejudices. What is needed is a feeling of urgency, of a new approach based on some very simple principle which I shall try to adumbrate.

The first is that temporary agreements and compensation assistance, desirable and laudable as they are, cannot solve the problem in the long run, but can only alleviate it. The only way to narrow the gap between the developed and developing nations is by industrialization and diversification of the economy of the emergent nations.

Two — This objective can be attained only through immense transfer of capital on a scale which would allow a break-through to self-sustained growth. Slow infiltration is futile, and in the long run a frontal attack on a large scale is much cheaper. With all the differences in skill, knowledge and experience, the rehabilitation of Europe through the Marshall Plan in a short concentrated period of time is clear proof of what can be achieved by a break-through.

My own country has proved again the possibility of a break-through, which was greatly assisted by the large import of capital resulting in a growth of 10 per cent per annum in the GNP in real terms during a period of 15 years. Without minimizing other factors and the special circumstances in Israel which make this fact possible, the import of capital was an essential precondition of the break-through.

Such a departure may involve some waste, but this is the price of solving the crucial problem of our century.

Three — The capacity of developing nations to absorb loans on commercial terms is limited and the conditions under which assistance is extended must be adapted to their capacity to repay, if such assistance is to be of any use.

Four — The economic transformation of the world cannot be carried into effect through the methods of "business as usual," and extraordinary efforts are required.

Five — Some ideas of the welfare state now applying to the internal relations in the developed nations must be projected to the global arena and made valid on an international scale as a guiding idea in relations between developing and industrialized nations.

If these guiding lines are disregarded, the efforts to narrow the gap between the two worlds will be a sisyphean labour, as it seems to be now in the light of past experience.

As already mentioned, of the $20 billion invested every year in the developing nations, only $4 billion represent net capital transfer from the industrialized nations. The task is to extend the scope of this transfer of capital so that it should be commensurate with the urgent needs of the underdeveloped nations. Moreover, such capital transfer must be implemented on terms and conditions under which a realistic projection of repayment would be possible. Much has been done in this field by the World Bank and the International Development Association, but the relationship between the challenge and the response is not satisfactory. The World Bank can lend only on commercial terms and its loans are hard loans as the funds of the World Bank are raised on commercial terms. Many of the developing nations can provide neither the collateral for hard loans nor borrow on terms which are too onerous for them. The International Development Association lends on terms well adapted to the capacity of the developing nations to assume financial obligations for their economic development, but the means at the disposal of the International Development Association are extremely limited.

The developing nations are already overburdened with debts on commercial terms and they can hardly meet the requirements of servicing such debts. The experience of my country, Israel, bears out how onerous the burden of interest payments can be. Thus, we are confronted with a dilemma that the terms of the World Bank are too difficult and the means of the International Development Association too limited. The flow of private capital does not increase and in the period 1956-1961 it stagnated at the rate of 2.5 billion dollars per annum, while the flow of governmental capital increased within the same period from $3 to 6 billion. This flow of governmental capital is an encouraging development which nobody would have dared to predict in 1956.

There are signs that the developed nations hesitate to increase, or even maintain, that pace of unilateral transfer of capital. However, capital could be mobilized on an adequate scale if the great potentialities on the free financial markets of the world were utilized.

This could be done if a guarantee of the developed nations were available. The advantages of such a guarantee instead of direct transfer of capital would be twofold: First of all, the difficulty of asking for direct budget allocations from the industrialized nations, which encounters tremendous difficulties, would be eliminated; secondly, if the bonds be sold in countries with a surplus in the balance of payments, there would be no immediate burden on the nations trying to straighten out their balance of payments. On the contrary, such financial activity would have an equilibrating effect. Thus, the objectives of the International Monetary

Fund and of the World Bank would dovetail in a most satisfactory manner. This solution would create not only international liquidity but, at the same time, additional global demand.

Under the present balance of payments situation, it would be much easier for the developed countries to provide such a guarantee as a long-term formal liability than to raise actual funds by budgetary allocation.

Credits extended to underdeveloped nations, if they are to be of any help at all, must be on conditions and at rates of interest substantially lower than those at which bonds can be sold on the financial markets, and more or less identical with the terms and conditions of the International Development Association. Therefore, an interest equalization fund of developed countries is indispensable in order to bridge the gap between the former and the latter conditions. [Editor's note: the equalization fund would, in effect, be an interest rate subsidy on loans to poor countries, paid by the rich countries.]

Relatively small amounts are involved, averaging about $40 million per annum per each billion dollars raised in that way. As nearly all of the developed countries extend grants to developing nations, in some cases the allocations to the Interest Equalization Fund could be deducted from these grants so that the total expenditure of the countries concerned would either in some cases increase very little or, in others, not at all. However, with the same amount an incomparably greater effect would be obtained by using them as an ignition spark to mobilize and release very large funds out of all proportion to the expenditure covering the interest differential.

Moreover, a suggestion which I had made at previous meetings of the Board of Governors of the World Bank, that surplus profits of the Bank, which do not need to be allocated to the already adequate reserves, should be transferred to the International Development Association, is now being approved. These are very substantial amounts which can form the basis for the Interest Equalization Fund if the Board of Governors of the World Bank approves of such a measure.

Consequently, the problem is one of security of bonds issued, scope of assistance made possible, and conditions under which credits could be extended.

The only way out of this dilemma seems to be the raising of funds on a commercial basis, with due consideration for international balance of payments problems and lending them on easy conditions. The bridge between these two sets of conditions would be a system of guarantees and an interest equalization fund. The quotas of the developed countries in the International Monetary Fund could provide the key to the distribution of the burden of guarantees. I would not like to deal with the institutional details of the plan, which could either be integrated with the World Bank and the International Development Association or based on a separate institution, although eventually the lending operation would be most effective through the International Development Association. Thus, the essentials of the plan are the following:

1. The funds would be raised without affecting the balance of payments of the nations concerned.

2. This objective could be attained if the funds are raised on a commercial basis through bonds sold on the market and if the bonds are always marketed in countries with surpluses in their balance of payments.

3. Such bonds must carry the guarantee properly and equitably distributed among the industrialized nations as a formal liability for a very long period of time. These guarantees most probably would come into effect only to a very small extent, or not at all, if the lending operations are effective in launching the developing nations on the road to a self-sustained economic growth.

4. The difference between rates of interest at which bonds could be sold and the interest on loans to the developing nations would be covered by an interest equalization fund raised by the whole developed world. The financial burden involved in the interest equalization fund for the developed world would be negligible.

5. Loans on the basis of these funds should be extended on conditions and terms identical with those presently applied by the International Development Association.

6. The capital raised in this way should be commensurate with the need of the developing world for an economic breakthrough.

7. In this way, the three main difficulties of assistance for the economic growth of the developing nations—the lack of sufficient collateral, the onerous conditions of credit, and the inadequate scope of assistance—would be overcome.

8. These measures would, at the same time, help in expanding the market for capital goods of industrialized nations, such industries being the key to the business cycle by bringing into use the presently unutilized capacity of production in some economically mature nations.

It seems that, with the means at the disposal of the world at the present moment, these problems are manageable.

This approach to the aid problem is admittedly a departure from the present routine. It requires courage and imagination, but it has the advantage of avoiding the danger of doing too little too late, and doing it in the wrong way.

An imaginative approach to the great problems of our century could have the same result that the counter-cyclical policy in the developed world had in the elimination of economic crises in the post-war world. Such a policy would not only narrow the gap between the two halves of humanity, but make richer and more prosperous all those embarking on this great venture.

THE NEED FOR ECONOMIC INTEGRATION AMONG UNDERDEVELOPED COUNTRIES (With Special Reference to Latin America)

Sidney Dell

The final major proposal at UNCTAD was to promote the economic integration of less developed countries with each other. In this chapter from a recent volume on the proposed Latin American Common Market, Sidney Dell, Director of the New York Office of UNCTAD, advances the case for a common market as well as some of the problems that arise in attempting to establish effective economic integration among developing countries. Although Mr. Dell's examples are based on Latin American conditions, they have a wider application to the problems of underdeveloped countries in general.

Stated in its simplest terms, the case for a common market in Latin America, as in any underdeveloped region, is that future economic growth presupposes a large amount of industrial development and that such development would be facilitated if the barriers to trade within the region could be reduced or eliminated.

While the importance of economies of scale is sometimes exaggerated, it seems clear that the national markets of most of the smaller underdeveloped countries are too restricted to provide an adequate volume of demand for mass-production industries. Productivity in any one country is likely to be lower the greater the number of different industrial products or varieties that it attempts to manufacture and the more its industries are limited to production for the home market alone. Where productivity is low and costs high, the tendency is for industry to seek —and obtain—correspondingly high protection. Yet if each industry in

Sidney Dell, "The Need for Economic Integration among Less-Developed Countries," excerpted from Sidney Dell, *A Latin American Common Market?* (New York: Oxford University Press under the auspices of the Royal Institute of International Affairs, 1966), pp. 15-35. Reprinted by permission of Oxford University Press and Sidney Dell.

each country is separately entitled to the amount of protection it requires to survive while operating under conditions of low output and high costs, the tendency to regional specialization is necessarily inhibited, and protected inefficiency within small self-contained markets becomes the rule.

Although Latin America is perhaps not as fragmented as Africa, many of the countries in the region are exceedingly small, whether in terms of area, population, or aggregate income. Out of the twenty Latin American republics, only five—Argentina, Brazil, Colombia, Mexico, and Peru—have populations over 10 million. Twelve of them have populations under 5 million. And to these may be added the three Guianas, each with less than 1 million inhabitants, and various islands of the Caribbean, almost all of which likewise have six-figure populations or less.

With their relatively low per capita incomes, the national markets of these countries are exceedingly small, and the purchasing power available after basic needs for food and shelter have been provided is still smaller. Even a country as large as Brazil, with about 80 million people, has a total income of the same order of magnitude as Australia and New Zealand with a combined population of only 14 million.[1]

The markets of most of these countries are much too small to permit the efficient operation of large-scale modern industry at anything like full capacity. That is why, side by side with an overall shortage of industrial capacity in relation to needs, most underdeveloped countries do not fully utilize even such limited capacity as they do have. Vast areas of land remain uncultivated, as already noted, while factories work their machinery at much less than optimum rates.

Thus, for example, only in two of the firms producing trucks in Brazil in 1961 did output exceed 50 per cent of the capacity of one shift, while in the other two firms the rate of utilization was less than 20 per cent of one shift. In cars, jeeps, and utility vehicles, two firms had utilization rates of 70 per cent of one-shift capacity.[2] It has to be borne in mind that two- or three-shift operation would be desirable in this particular industry.

Similar situations are to be found in other industries and other countries. In Mexico, for example, it was estimated that in 1962 most in-

[1] As noted earlier, inter-country comparisons of national income are subject to serious limitations, and comparisons of the above type, between developed and underdeveloped countries, may be particularly misleading. In the present context, however, the comparison has a certain validity, being designed to throw light on the total money income available for purchases of industrial products.

[2] ECLA, *Problemas y perspectivas del desarrollo industrial latinoamericano* (E/CN.12/664, Apr. 1963), 29.

dustrial establishments were operating at something like 50 per cent of capacity.[3] It is likely that even lower operating ratios are characteristic of the smaller Latin American countries, and that a situation of this sort must be a serious deterrent to investment in new capacity. The discouragement to new investment must be particularly serious in those branches of industry where even a single plant of optimum size would have no prospect of access to a market large enough to ensure economical rates of operation. This is certainly the case for all the many countries and islands in the Western Hemisphere with populations under 5 million.

But, it may be asked, why should it be necessary for Colombia, with a population of 15 million, to join an economic union, when Switzerland, a country with only one-third of Colombia's population, has been able to achieve a very high *per capita* income without being a member of an economic union? *A fortiori,* what compelling reasons can there be for countries like Argentina (22 million), Mexico (40 million), and Brazil (80 million) to seek economic integration with their neighbours? The answer is that Switzerland embarked upon its economic development at a time when international trade was still relatively free, and the establishment of new industries could take into account the existence of markets abroad as well as at home. Far different is the present situation confronting the underdeveloped countries. Few of them, in establishing manufacturing industries at the present time, could count on significant export markets. Markets in the industrial countries are closed to them, partly because by now the technological lag is so great that, even though wages in underdeveloped countries are much lower, total costs per unit of output are generally higher because of such factors as low productivity of labour, lack of complementary facilities, or high costs of raw materials, power, or transport: and partly because wherever this is not so, the industrial countries take steps to protect themselves against so-called unfair competition. On the other hand, markets in other underdeveloped countries are also closed to them. Where other underdeveloped countries have competing industries of their own, they have generally protected them in the home market up to the hilt. And where they do not have competing industries of their own, they would rather buy low-cost imports from North America and Western Europe than high-cost imports from their neighbours.

In general, where underdeveloped countries have gained their economic independence, their immediate reaction has often been to asso-

[3] Estimate by the president of the Confederation of Industrial Associations of Mexico, cited in *Comercio Exterior,* March 1963, 138-40.

ciate political nationalism with economic nationalism, and to try and go it alone over the whole range of industry. Moreover, once a broad and comprehensive system of protection has been introduced, the international rule of non-discrimination has prevented any liberalization *vis-à-vis* other underdeveloped countries.

THE INDUSTRIAL PROBLEM OF LATIN AMERICA

During the very first stage of industrial development, this kind of constriction of the channels of trade does not necessarily impede growth to a major extent. Most of the Latin American countries have been able to establish substantial consumer goods industries without looking for markets beyond their own frontiers: and in many of these countries nearly all domestic requirements for manufactured consumer goods are now satisfied from home production.

By the same token, however, these countries have now reached, or are closely approaching, the limit of import saving that is possible in the light industries: and the rate of investment and the growth of income generated in these industries must therefore begin to slow down if it has not already done so. New impetus to industrial investment and expansion, and new opportunities for closing the external gap by import saving will have to come from the development of industries manufacturing intermediate products such as steel and chemicals, as well as durable producer and consumer goods.

There has been a growing consciousness in recent years of the vulnerability of underdeveloped countries that arises from their dependence on the exchange of exported primary commodities for imported manufactures: and this has been accompanied by general acceptance of the need for diversification of production and exports in these countries. What is still not widely understood is that even the industry of these countries is also usually of a semi-colonial or dependent character. For it consists mainly, in most cases, of the elementary processing of crude foodstuffs or raw materials for export to the industrial countries: and of the production of certain relatively simple types of consumer goods, possibly coupled with the final assembly or finishing stages of certain other products, based on imported components. As such, the industry of underdeveloped countries lacks the very simplest and indispensable requirement of independent life—namely the capacity to reproduce itself.

From this standpoint, the industrial development of the at present underdeveloped countries has followed a course somewhat different from that of Western Europe and North America. The Industrial Revolution in Britain meant not only the mechanization of textile production but also the manufacture of the new types of power-generating machinery that were needed in industry and transport. The growth of factory production of consumer goods went hand in hand with the building of mechanical and engineering industries. The same pattern of development was subsequently followed in the United States and on the continent of Europe. Later still in the countries of Eastern Europe, the Soviet Union, and China it was recognized that machine-building industries were the foundation of a self-supporting economy: the emphasis on heavy industry was probably excessive in the early years of development, and too little attention was given to opportunities for specialization and exchange. But the essential approach was based on valid inferences from the past experience of the developed market economies of North America and Western Europe.

It is the lack of machine-building and other intermediate industries that makes the industrial economies of many of the underdeveloped countries so exceptionally vulnerable to the vagaries of the world market for primary commodities. Since machinery and intermediate goods (metal products, chemicals, and other heavy industry products) have largely to be imported, a decline in foreign exchange resources resulting from a downturn in demand for primary commodities reacts immediately on the ability of underdeveloped countries to buy imported materials and equipment.

In the dialogue between the developed and underdeveloped countries, spokesmen for the former are apt to argue that if only the latter would "put their houses in order," consume less and save more, their problems could be solved. There is no doubt much force in the contention that underdeveloped countries have done far less for themselves than they could have done, and that they may sometimes be tempted to blame others for what are really their own failings. Equally, however, it would be quite false to suppose that attempts to save more in underdeveloped countries would necessarily lead to higher investment and growth. For so long as an expansion of investment presupposes larger imports of machinery from developed countries: and so long as larger imports of machinery depend in turn on a corresponding rise in earnings from exports to (or in financial aid from) the developed countries: and so long, finally, as the latter countries cannot or will not undertake to provide the larger markets or financial aid thus required—so long must any attempts to mobilize additional savings in underdeveloped countries be frustrated by the inability to translate such savings into new productive capacity.

Thus the stagnation of trade between developed and underdeveloped countries has made it essential for the latter countries to stop relying on their traditional pattern of industrial growth, and to seek a more balanced expansion of all the major branches of industry. By this means they may be able to reduce the sensitivity of their economies to outside disturbances while increasing their own potential growth. At the same time, however, the very small national markets of most of these countries make it necessary for them to seek joint development of those industries in which economies of scale and of regional specialization may be significant. For however reasonable it may be for small countries to set up industries producing tinned food products, or finished textiles, or footwear, within the limits of their own home markets, they are bound to be at a serious disadvantage in undertaking the large-scale investments required for many sectors of heavy industry.

As we have seen, light consumer goods industries are already to be found in all Latin American countries, supplying in many cases virtually the whole range of domestic requirements in the products concerned. Capital goods industries, on the other hand, are still in their infancy, although they have by now attained some significance in Argentina, Brazil, and Mexico. In the case of Brazil, some two-thirds of the machinery and equipment used are manufactured in the country itself: the proportion is somewhat smaller in Argentina, and much smaller in Mexico.[4] Brazil would, in fact, be much closer than it is to establishing a capacity for growth independent of outside forces had it not failed thus far to solve the problem of its food and fuel supplies, which use up much of its available foreign exchange. But apart from Brazil, and to a lesser extent Argentina and Mexico, Latin America remains a heavily dependent region as far as the capacity for industrial expansion is concerned.

Some headway has been made in recent years in durable consumer goods industries, which have been growing rapidly in Argentina, Brazil, Chile, Colombia, Mexico, Peru, Uruguay, and Venezuela. In all these cases, however, little or no provision has been made for regional trade. The situation has become particularly serious in the automobile industry, which has already developed rapidly in Argentina, Brazil, and Mexico, while similar development is under way in Chile, Colombia, Peru, and Venezuela.

[4] ECLA, *Problemas y perspectivas del desarrollo industrial,* 17.

The sort of problem raised by fragmentation of the Latin American market is strikingly illustrated in this industry: data have already been cited on the low rate of capacity utilization in Brazil. The total market represented by the above seven countries exceeds 300,000 passenger cars and 250,000 trucks per annum at the present time. The production of these vehicles is already carried on by about sixty firms, and new factories or assembly plants are under consideration. Yet the above total market is smaller than that available to such European firms as Fiat (566,000 units per annum), Opel (360,000), Renault (350,000), and Ford of Britain (330,000). As against these latter figures, the largest-scale output for a single firm in Latin America is 20,000 units for trucks and 50,000 for cars.[5]

Available studies of the passenger car industry suggest that cost reductions associated with increasing scale of operations are particularly important up to an annual output of 50,000 units. It will therefore be obvious that most of the Latin American motor vehicle producers are operating on a scale at which unit costs tend to fall rather rapidly as output rises.

It has nevertheless proved extremely difficult to secure any co-operation between countries in the development of this industry. Indeed, some countries, notably Argentina and Brazil, have created a vast amount of unnecessary *internal* duplication of capacity. This has been done by offering such favourable terms and facilities to European and American producers that the latter were able to set up a whole series of local plants almost without regard to the efficiency of operations, with a virtual guarantee that their investment would pay off handsomely.

Another striking example of failure to exploit the economies of scale is to be found in the chemical industry. At the present time Latin America produces about 70 per cent of the chemicals it consumes. An extensive study of the industry by the Secretariat of ECLA has shown that if production were organized on a regional scale, the Latin American countries could bring their prices down below international levels. For example, it is estimated that the chemical industry could bring its prices down to 18 per cent below international prices in Colombia, 14 per cent in Mexico, 10 per cent in Brazil, 9 per cent in Peru, 6 per cent in Argentina, 2 per cent in Chile, and 1 per cent in Venezuela.[6]

The waste, inefficiency, and duplication of the automobile and chemical industries in Latin America are typical of the problems that arise

[5] ECLA, *Problemas y perspectivas del desarrollo industrial*, p. 141.

[6] ECLA, *La industria química de Latinoamérica* (UN Sales No. 64.II.G.7), 1963, Table 106.

because industries are being built up behind the walls of national protection without regard to the prospects for long-run viability, or the needs and resources of the continent as a whole.

PROXIMATE FACTORS IN LATIN AMERICAN INTEGRATION

The underlying rationale of economic integration in Latin America will now be clear, the main consideration being that access to a region-wide market would make it possible to take advantage of important economies of scale and regional specialization: and this would not merely contribute to more efficient operation of existing industries but would create additional incentives for the establishment of new industries and thus help to speed up the rate of growth. . . .

* * *

The negotiations that led ultimately to the signing of the Treaty of Montevideo,* in February 1960, began with quite limited objectives in August 1958 with consultations among experts from four countries only —Argentina, Brazil, Chile, and Uruguay. These countries had for some time previously been trading with one another on a preferential basis, and their mutual trade accounted in fact for the major part of total trade within the Latin American region.

The system of trade between these countries was not based on a preferential system of tariffs, but rather on the employment of exchange and trade controls in a selective manner. For example, Brazil would allocate foreign exchange for imports of fruit from Argentina or Chile and not for corresponding imports from other countries. And Argentina and Chile would reciprocate in their own import policies.

* * *

The question consequently arose—how could the channels of trade that had been developed under the previous system of discriminatory import and exchange controls be preserved? Thus the practical search for some immediate means of restoring the flow of trade between the four South American countries: Argentina, Brazil, Chile, and Uruguay, coincided with the attempt, on a broader plane and with longer-range objectives, to bring about a greater measure of economic co-operation and even integration within Latin America as a whole. It was, moreover,

[* Which established a Latin American free trade area as a possible initial basis for a future common market.]

natural for these two sets of objectives to come together, and for common ground to be sought between them.

* * *

At later meetings during 1959, and finally at the meeting at which the Treaty of Montevideo was completed and signed, further steps were taken to broaden the original draft Agreement by including provisions regarding the more permanent objectives of the participating countries. Existing trade among the southern group consisted largely of primary products, while the greatest potential for economic co-operation was likely to lie, as we have seen, in the development of industries on the basis of access to region-wide markets. It was thus necessary to merge the preservation of existing trade with provision for the development of new types of trade, especially in industrial goods.

* * *

THE SCOPE OF REGIONAL CO-OPERATION AND THE HEMISPHERE

Why did the Treaty not go further and allow for economic integration on a hemisphere-wide basis? We may pause for a moment on this point before going on to examine the Treaty itself.

No major initiative for economic union with the United States has thus far emerged in Latin America.[7] The idea of such a union has, however, often been suggested in the United States. Indeed, the concept of a Western Hemisphere economic union has probably been gaining ground in the United States in recent years. Such a concept runs directly counter to traditional United States foreign economic policy which has generally sought to gain universal acceptance of the idea of non-discrimination, and the ending of preferential systems such as those of the Commonwealth or the French Community. Throughout the Second World War the United States tried to persuade Britain to do away with Commonwealth preference, and accepted the preservation of the system after the war only with the greatest reluctance.

The special economic relationships prevailing within the Commonwealth have in fact been very much loosened by postwar developments,

[7] In August 1957, at an economic conference of the OAS in Buenos Aires, Peru proposed the establishment of "a permanent inter-American commission for the Western Hemisphere common market." All other Latin American countries, however, favoured exclusively Latin American regional or subregional common markets. But see the statement by Dr. Prebisch cited at the end of this chapter.

and a similar tendency may be observed within the French Community, although there the loosening process has not yet gathered momentum. Indeed, despite the establishment of the European Economic Community and the accession of the former French African colonies to political independence, a considerable—and thus far fairly successful—effort has been made to develop a new form of association between the latter countries and the EEC as a whole.

American interest in a Western Hemisphere economic union may be viewed, in part, as a response to the attempt of the EEC to create the basis for a union between Western Europe and Africa. If the EEC builds Eurafrica, and if Britain seeks a tightening of Commonwealth ties once more, why should not the United States, it may be asked, draw the obvious conclusions regarding its own position in the Western Hemisphere?

* * *

There now began to be signs that there were Latin Americans who might consider some exclusive trading arrangement with the United States in retaliation against the discriminatory features of the association of certain African countries with the EEC. The Secretariat of the ECLA commented significantly that

> If it turned out that the EEC system of preferences for African countries must inevitably be renewed, this would be regarded as a precedent that might perhaps enable Latin America to initiate negotiations with the United States for the ultimate establishment of some form of preference in the United States market for certain articles of great actual or potential importance in the balance of payments of Latin American countries.[8]

In October 1963 the Secretariat of the OAS in Washington suggested that while Latin American countries were aware of the shortcomings of regional preferential arrangements, it was likely to take a long time before a more general system of preferences for developing countries could be organized, because of the reluctance of African countries to give up their existing privileged access to the British or EEC market. In these circumstances, the OAS Secretariat proposed that the United States should make unilateral tariff concessions to Latin American countries for products on which the latter were themselves lowering their mutual trade barriers within the framework of their regional groupings[9] (i.e. LAFTA and the Central American common market).

[8] UN, *Acontecimientos y tendencias recientes en el intercambio de América Latina con la Communidad Económica Europea,* July 22, 1962, p. 44.

[9] OEA/CIES/369, Oct. 19, 1963 (Spanish text, 12).

This was followed by endorsement of the idea of a Western Hemisphere common market by an influential Subcommittee of the United States Congress:

While the concept of a fully developed Western Hemisphere common market seems, at the moment, distant and fenced in by nationalism, it holds a sufficient hope for advancing the economy and industrialization of Latin America and the entire hemisphere to deserve the study of trade experts everywhere.[10]

And the growing independence of Western Europe led Senator Hubert Humphrey to a similar conclusion:

The emergence of a powerful Western Europe—likely to pursue a more independent foreign policy—makes hemisphere co-operation more urgent if the nations of this hemisphere are not only to solve their immediate internal problems but to play a proper role in world affairs in future decades. . . . Trade is essential to the economic prosperity of the hemisphere and we should give careful consideration to the possibility of developing a more cohesive trading area, which would not only bring economic advantages but would also promote the political unity of the hemisphere.[11]

Despite the various indications of growing interest in the possibility of a Western Hemisphere preferential system, it seems unlikely that such a system will ultimately commend itself either to the Latin American countries or to the United States. The Latin American countries could never accept the Rockefeller proposal for "a free flow of men and goods and money from Point Barrow to Tierra del Fuego" because this would mean complete freedom for United States firms to compete with, and probably overwhelm, the new industries of the region.

The Latin American countries would no doubt be greatly tempted by any United States offer to grant non-reciprocal preferences to imports from Latin America, especially if it became clear that African countries were unwilling to agree to the scaling down, progressively, of the prefer-

[10] US Congress, Joint Economic Committee, *Private Investment in Latin America*, a Report of the Subcommittee on Inter-American Economic Relationships (OEA/CIES/369) (1964), 25.

[11] Senator Hubert H. Humphrey, "US Policy in Latin America," *Foreign Affairs*, July 1964. The article was published before Senator Humphrey received the nomination of the Democratic Party for Vice-President of the United States. In his article, Senator Humphrey suggested that the first step in promoting "a hemispheric trade zone" might be for the United States to lend strong support to the development of LAFTA. Once LAFTA had made significant progress, it would be possible to consider what new trade relationships should be developed between the LAFTA area and the United States and Canada.

ences they now enjoy in Western Europe. But an arrangement of this sort seems unlikely. For one thing, it is difficult to imagine such an offer being made without any *quid pro quo* of any kind, and the question of the acceptability of such a *quid pro quo* to the Latin American countries would then arise.

On the other hand, the United States, as the leading world power, is likely to ponder carefully the limitations on its influence in Africa, Asia, and indeed, Europe that might follow the introduction of discriminatory ties with Latin America. It would be against the interests of a dominant industrial power to accept any arrangements that would tend to limit its access to any part of the world market: it would thus generally prefer an open system of relatively free trade on a world-wide basis to any restricted system or grouping. Political factors might likewise deter a major world power from granting exclusive privileges to a particular group of countries so long as it wished to retain influence with other groups.[12]

These considerations do not rule out the possibility of some form of special Western Hemisphere programme of economic co-operation: indeed, the Alliance for Progress is just such a programme, providing for the United States to grant financial aid to Latin American countries for the achievement of certain development goals. For the United States to go further and give exclusive privileges to Latin America would imply taking an essentially pessimistic view of the prospects for its future relationships with the Commonwealth and the EEC: and for the Latin American countries to accept such privileges would mean running the risk of creating a dependent relationship, and, if reciprocity were conceded, endangering the prosperity of their newly established industries as well.

A preferential system limited to the Western Hemisphere would also reverse one of the major achievements of the United Nations Conference on Trade and Development of 1964. At that conference it was unanimously agreed that existing preferential arrangements between developed and underdeveloped countries should be abolished *pari passu* with the granting of at least equivalent advantages (in the form of additional aid or market outlets) to the underdeveloped countries at present participating in such arrangements.[13] There is thus a danger of undoing the

[12] Nevertheless, *Business Week* reported on Jan. 23, 1965 that the State Department was looking 'again' at the question of US trade preferences for Latin America. It was suggested that if the Kennedy Round failed to produce significant European concessions to Latin America, US pressure for a US-Latin American preferential system would grow.

[13] UNCTAD, *Proceedings, i.,* 30.

progress made at the Geneva Conference in bringing to an end what was essentially a survival of the old colonial systems of economy.

As Dr. Raúl Prebisch put the matter in an address to the United Nations Trade and Development Board on April 6, 1965:

One of the main reasons why developing countries have recognized the need to diversify not only the composition but also the destination of their exports is so that they may not have to depend on a single great country or group of countries, but may be able to trade with the entire world. I think that that is of the greatest importance from the political point of view. Unfortunately, there are some symptoms that the spirit of Geneva is not being applied, and that on the contrary there is an aggravation of the tendency towards a system of discriminatory preferences in certain parts of the world. I cannot hide from the Board my great concern at signs in certain Latin American circles, which are manifesting themselves with increasing force in requests to the United States for a preferential system to be exclusive to Latin American countries. I believe that that is contrary to the spirit of Geneva, and I consider it my duty to call the Board's attention to it. For what Governments do in the near future in this respect may not be of a temporary nature; it will have a tremendous impact on the character and shape of the economic future of the world. Those decisions will mean either the establishment of a new pattern of world integration and world economic unity or the establishment of new forms of disintegration of the world by segmentation into zones of influence covering some developed countries and a group of developing countries.[14]

[14] TD/B/9.